School Librarian's Grade-by-Grade Activities Program

School Librarian's Grade-by-Grade Activities Program

A Complete Sequential Skills Plan for Grades K-8

Carol Collier Kuhlthau, M.L.S.

The Center for Applied Research in Education, Inc.
West Nyack, New York

Library of Congress Cataloging in Publication Data

Kuhlthau, Carol C. (Carol Collier)
  School librarian's grade-by-grade activities
program.

  1. Libraries and schools—United States.
2. Education, Elementary—United States—
Curricula. I. Title.
Z718.K83   025.5'678222   81-10121
ISBN 0-87628-744-5   AACR2

Printed in the United States of America

About the Author

Carol Collier Kuhlthau has been an elementary school teacher and a school library media specialist at both the elementary and high school levels. She is currently the library media specialist at the Lawrence Brook Elementary School in East Brunswick, New Jersey.

Mrs. Kuhlthau earned her M.L.S. from Rutgers University in New Brunswick, New Jersey, and is a doctoral candidate at the Rutgers Graduate School of Education. Her areas of concentration are the effects of television on learning of young children, and library and information skills instruction.

Preface

This book provides a comprehensive, sequential activities program for developing basic library and information skills. For easy use, it is organized into eight chapters which match the developmental stages and specific needs of children at each of the following levels:

- Readiness (Kindergarten)
- First Grade
- Second Grade
- Third Grade
- Fourth Grade
- Fifth Grade
- Sixth Grade
- Advanced (Seventh and Eighth Grades)

Each chapter gives the library media specialist detailed guidelines and activities for building sequential skills at a particular level, including a discussion of the characteristics and library needs of children, a sequential skills checklist, and a variety of ready-to-use activities for teaching the skills at that level. The activities are designed for use with a class-size group of children who are at approximately the same level, as most library media specialists instruct such classes on a regular basis.

The library skills activities at each grade level include all of the directions needed for successful use. Each activity provides the following:

- A title keyed to a specific skill on the checklist at the particular grade level
- An introduction that spells out the purpose of the activity
- The time required to complete the activity
- A list of materials needed for the activity
- Clear, concise directions for presenting the activity
- Suggestions for variations or supplementary activities

The checklists of skills to be learned by children at each grade level provide a simple record of instruction. The checklists may be used to record the progress of classes or individuals. However they are used, they will help you provide a continuity of skills instruction from grade to grade.

This sequential instructional program is meant to be integrated with the content areas of the curriculum and should be supplemented by extensive individual use of the library media center. It represents a new and practical way to strengthen and revitalize library skills instruction. It may be incorporated into the skills instruction you are now using or it may serve as the basis for an entirely new instructional program.

Carol C. Kuhlthau

Contents

V.   FOURTH GRADE: Using the Library Media Center Independently **89**

The Fourth Grade Program (89)

The Card Catalog • Dewey Decimal System • Research and Reporting Techniques • Working in Groups • Using the Library Media Center Collection • Reading • Book Logs • Kinds of Fiction—Mystery and Fantasy • Television and Reading • Summary

Fourth Grade Library Skills Checklist and Activities (97)

Library Skills Checklist: FOURTH GRADE (98)

CONTENTS

School Librarian's Grade-by-Grade Activities Program

About This Library Skills Activities Program

The following describes the basis for the sequential library skills program in this book and points out the special features of the program. It should help you put these materials to most effective use in your own library media center.

THE BASIS FOR THE PROGRAM

The program was designed by analyzing the library skills capabilities of children at each stage of their development and then matching these capabilities to appropriate activities. Research done in the first half of the century, especially the extensive studies of the Swiss psychologist Jean Piaget, defined some specific stages in cognitive growth. The description of these stages makes it possible to determine how well students at a certain age will comprehend a lesson.

For example, before the age of six or seven, children are generally unable to understand tasks that require categorizing and classification. At this stage, therefore, detailed instruction in the Dewey Decimal System would be futile and possibly even destructive to later learning. Similarly, abilities that enable one to do research, such as combining data from a number of sources into a cohesive whole, are not fully developed until the ages of twelve to sixteen. Thus, research assignments given to younger children must take this fact into consideration.

A chart of Piaget's stages of cognitive development with brief descriptions of the abilities of children, which particularly pertain to library and information skills, follows. The stages and accompanying abilities are further explained in the corresponding grade sections.

Piaget's Stages of Cognitive Development

   Sensory Motor—Birth to Age 2

   Learns through senses and movement.

   Preoperational—Ages 2-7

   Can use symbols to represent reality, such as language.
   Has an egocentric point of view.

   Concrete Operational—Ages 7-11

   Can perform mental operations on a concrete level.
   Can categorize and use classification.
   Is not capable of abstract thinking.

   Formal Operational—Ages 12-16

   Can use abstract thought.
   Can generalize.
   Can form a hypothesis.

The program also attempts to incorporate the most natural ways children learn at each stage and owes much in this respect to the philosophy and approach to instruction of James Moffett.* It attempts to take into account the physical, emotional, and social development of children, as well as their cognitive needs.

For instance, at certain stages children learn well in groups and with partners. At other stages they need to do more individual work. At all ages, children learn better by participating in an activity than they do by merely listening to a teacher's explanation. They also need opportunities to understand their mistakes and to correct errors promptly.

THE NATURE OF THE ACTIVITIES

The activities in each section of this library and information skills program are designed for active student participation. They are planned with the least possible amount of teacher talk. The library media specialist provides the setting, introduction, and procedure to be followed and also provides guidance along the way. The students take an active part in their own learning through participation in the activities.

The activities are planned to correspond to the way the skill will be used in the library media center. Whenever possible, the students use an actual source instead of talking about it or filling in a worksheet about it. Worksheets are helpful for review and practice, but there is no substitute for going to the actual source and using it.

Many of the activities are planned for small groups or partners. This provides both the opportunity for children to learn from each other and a social

---

*See his *Student-Centered Language Arts and Reading, K-13* (Boston: Houghton Mifflin, 1976).

experience that makes the task more desirable. Games are also used to add incentive to necessary reviewing tasks.

Correction of error is built into the activities as often as possible. The objective of these activities is for children to learn from their mistakes, not to be graded for their performance. Most of the activities allow students to correct their mistakes by providing prompt feedback on their progress.

The activities are intended to be examples of the kind of lessons you can use to teach skills at each level. Please do not hesitate to adapt them in any way to serve your particular needs or to create your own activities for presenting skills. Often the most successful learning takes place when we plan an activity for a specific group of students. Each of us is the expert on the children in our own school, the library media center collection, and the nature of our community. Our enthusiasm for an activity can stir the interest and motivation of students that are essential for successful learning.

THE SEQUENTIAL STRUCTURE

This program provides a sequence for children to learn library and information skills. These skills and concepts build on each other in a hierarchical way. One skill aids the learning of other, more difficult skills. Through regular use of the program, library skills are gradually developed from the readiness through the advanced levels.

Although it is important to maintain the sequence of skills, you may determine the pace at which the students move through the sequence. Not all children or groups of children will neatly fit into the designated grade-level stages. Some will advance quickly while others will linger behind. Thus, pace the sequence at a rate compatible with the majority of the students in your school. Supplement with individual and small group instruction for students who need additional practice to master certain skills. Many of the activities include suggestions for reinforcing the particular skill learned.

The skills sequence is structured so that students will learn the basic library skills by the end of elementary school or the completion of the sixth grade. The consistent instruction needed to build these skills may be provided on a regularly scheduled basis throughout the elementary grades. In this way, a foundation is provided for individual, independent use of the library media center at the secondary level.

THE LIBRARY SKILLS CHECKLISTS

The Library Skills Checklist in each grade-level section lists the specific library and information skills to be learned at the particular level. As each skill is taught, using the suggested activities or others of your own choice, you can check off the corresponding skill on the checklist or record the date of instruction. This will enable you to keep a continuous record of the progression of instruction at all levels.

The checklists may also be used to record individual progress in a particular skill that has been difficult to develop or to record the progress of a particular class at a specific stage in the program. For example, recording the individual progress of students in a sixth grade class in review activities will help you determine which ones need further instruction.

The Library Skills Sequential Skill Plan chart accompanying this aid traces the complete library skills progression through all eight levels, readiness through advanced. It provides a quick visual reference to aid you in planning your own program and in working with teachers.

INTEGRATION WITH THE CURRICULUM

Library and information skills are not separate school subjects. Like reading and writing, they are *process skills*—skills used to reach other learning goals. We read to derive meaning. We write to convey thoughts. We use library skills to locate and interpret materials that expand our understanding and better enable us to make decisions and choices. When process skills are taught as isolated subjects, learning problems, such as lack of motivation, retention, and transference, often result.

Instruction in library and information skills should be integrated into the school curriculum. The sequence of skills may be closely tied to instruction and learning in the content areas of the curriculum. Activities in the subject areas should require students to use the library media center and the corresponding skills that are being acquired at each level in the library and information sequence.

Integrating the library media center program with classroom instruction requires joint planning between the library media specialist and the teacher. Each grade-level section in this aid provides specific suggestions for effective mutual planning and team teaching. Recommendations of particular skills to be coordinated are also made. Provision for integration of the library skills program with subject areas gradually increases with each grade until the library media center program is completely coordinated with the curriculum of the school at the secondary level. This process begins at the readiness, or kindergarten, level when the library program consists mostly of storytelling, with only an occasional connection with classroom instruction, and culminates with the advanced level when the library media program consists mostly of research and reporting emanating from the classroom.

LOCATION AND INTERPRETATION SKILLS

Library and information skills fall into two broad categories: the location of materials and the interpretation of materials. Location skills help children to understand how materials are organized to make it possible to locate some information or a particular material. This is the information science approach to library skills instruction.

In the intermediate grades, children analyze the Dewey Decimal System as a model of one way to organize materials and the card catalog as an index to the library media center collection. The library media center becomes a laboratory for students to learn the concepts of information organization and retrieval. At the advanced level, students consider other ways to organize and retrieve information. They compare Library of Congress cataloging with the Dewey Decimal System and the use of computers with the card catalog. Through the use of indexes, they become aware of the network of library services.

The information science approach helps students to understand the sources of information available to them and enables them to locate the materials and information that they need. This approach to library skills instruction prepares students to transfer their ability to locate materials in the library media center to other libraries and information storage systems.

Interpretation skills help students understand and use the materials that are located. Although library media specialists have traditionally taught only location skills, we have been more involved in the interpretation of materials than has been acknowledged. We help children understand and use library media center materials starting with the earliest storytelling experiences at the kindergarten level and continuing on to research experiences at the advanced level.

One approach used in this library skills program is to help children understand materials from the "inside." This is accomplished by giving them opportunities to take the role of the author in producing their own materials. In the primary grades, students use the three D's—discussion, dramatization, and drawing—to relate what they have heard and seen to their own experiences. When their reading and writing skills have improved, they are given opportunities to make their own books and to write their own stories.

Other activities to help children find meaning in what they read and view are also included for each grade. Book logs are kept to record reactions to reading. Advertising posters are designed and best-seller lists compiled to share favorite books with others. Book talks are given to expand children's awareness of available materials.

Research and reporting techniques require extensive understanding and interpretation of library media center materials. The activities suggested in this area give children early opportunities to react to materials by recalling, summarizing, and paraphrasing what they see and hear. In the intermediate grades, students extend these skills by adding their own ideas, experiences, and information gathered from outside sources. In the upper grades, students have opportunities to apply their increasing ability to recall, summarize, paraphrase, and extend in research and reporting in subject areas of the curriculum.

The program also provides students with practical suggestions for gathering information from various sources and combining it into a cohesive report. These are difficult skills that the student is not fully capable of until the advanced level, but some useful techniques are introduced at earlier grades to build a foundation for later success.

Through the library and information program, children are also helped to understand and interpret influential information sources outside of the library media center. Television is a dominant information source in our environment and warrants consideration in the library skills program. Each grade-level section provides activities to develop listening and viewing skills to help children understand, evaluate, and select media for information and entertainment. Through these and other activities, children increase their understanding of the difference between reading and viewing. They become more aware of different types of television programs and are encouraged to discuss what they view and extend television programs through library media center materials.

OVERALL OBJECTIVE
OF THE LIBRARY SKILLS PROGRAM

The overall objective of the library and information skills program is to help children make satisfying choices of media for information and entertainment. The sequential program provides children with an understanding of the information available to them, the skills to locate desired materials, and the ability to intelligently evaluate, select, and interpret materials.

I. READINESS

Preparing Children to Use the Library Media Center

During their first year of school, young children will need to learn what a library is and be prepared to use the library media center. They will be introduced to a wide variety of materials and have experience functioning as a group. They will also learn the routines and procedures of the library media center.

This chapter provides:

- A description of kindergartners' needs in terms of the library program
- A checklist of library skills to be developed at the readiness level
- Activities for teaching specific skills on the checklist

THE READINESS PROGRAM

When five-year-olds come to school, they have not all had the same opportunities to experience libraries and books. Some kindergarten children have been to the public library, have had experience with borrowing books, and have even attended storytelling sessions. Others have had little experience with libraries, but have books of their own and have been read to at home. Unfortunately, there are also children who have had few opportunities to come in contact with books and little experience with being read stories.

It is important to assess the experience of the children in your school to determine the extent and depth of the readiness program needed. You need not feel bound by the grade-level differentiations presented in this book. Adapt the readiness program to the background experience and needs of the children in your school. Some children will need a readiness program that continues on into the first grade, while others will move on quickly to the next level of activities.

The program presented here provides the sequence of library and information skills instruction. You determine the pace appropriate for the students in your school.

Storytelling and Story Reading

The central function of the readiness program consists of reading a wide variety of interesting storybooks to children. This is a rewarding, enjoyable experience for both children and library media specialists. In order to provide the richest possible environment for listening to a story, it is helpful to understand some of the behavior and characteristics that five-year-olds typically display.

Getting Attention

Getting the attention of an entire class of five-year-olds is often difficult. To read a story you must have everyone sitting quietly and ready to listen. This is no simple task with most kindergarten classes.

At this age, children are individualistic and self-centered. They have a limited interest in what their classmates are doing or thinking. They are naturally active and want to be involved in whatever captures their attention at the time. This may not necessarily be what the class is doing or what you have planned for them. They want to please adults and are generally affectionate. They need the warmth and security derived from the adults around them. Five-year-olds especially enjoy individual attention. They work best alone or in very small groups.

Five-year-olds don't respond well to terms that address the class as a whole, such as "everyone," "children," or "boys and girls." It is important to learn their names as rapidly as possible. Call individual children by name to get their attention and to have them settle down so they can listen to a story. This, of course, does not mean that you will need to call out all of the names, but it will be helpful for you to call the names of several children who are distracted and paying attention to something else.

Next, establish a routine. Five-year-olds enjoy the security of repetition. Develop a simple pattern for them to follow and they will soon comply with only a gentle urging. For instance, have the children sit in the same place and follow the same procedure to get ready for listening to a story each time that they come to the library media center.

Use of an attention-getting device is often an effective way to get children ready to listen to a story. Some attention-getting devices are finger plays, songs, exercises, and puppets. The use of such devices should be established as a signal to settle down for a story and should not be varied too much from session to session. The following simple exercise works well: Have the children stretch their arms high over their heads, wiggle their fingers around, and bring their hands slowly down into their laps. Whatever you use should be quieting and simple, designed to prepare the children for listening. Avoid attention-getting devices that become a distraction in themselves.

Choosing Books for Story Reading

Once the children are ready to listen and you have begun the story, the children's attention usually becomes quite intense. The attention of five-year-olds is concentrated but of relatively short duration. Choose books that tell a vivid, yet simple story. Avoid stories that are too subtle or overly long. It is important to make the most of the children's attention before their interest wanes. This highly concentrated attention, like any other vigorous activity, quickly results in fatigue. By giving careful consideration to the way five-year-olds use attention, you can make storytelling a rich, enjoyable experience.

Sharing Ideas About a Story

One of the most enjoyable and productive outcomes of listening to a story with a group is sharing reactions to the story. This is not something that simply happens. It can be gradually cultivated throughout the elementary school years. Although children at this age are very alert, eager to learn, and ready to respond, their language and speech skills are limited. Most learning at this level is nonverbal, taking place through manipulating concrete objects and imaginative play. Language ability will vary among the children, as do other abilities. Some children are shy and especially limited in ways of expressing ideas and feelings. The background experience of the individual child will affect his or her ability to use language to express thoughts.

Five-year-olds have difficulty sticking to a point during a discussion. They are unfamiliar with the dynamics of group talk. Being more accustomed to one-to-one conversation, they will blurt out whatever pops into their heads at the time. They lack experience in discussions centering on one topic. Their spontaneous, uninhibited talk wanders from one fleeting thought to another.

Another characteristic of five-year-olds is that their perspective is self-centered. This does not mean that they are inconsiderate of others, but rather that they think that everyone has the same point of view as they have. This makes it difficult for them to listen to what others have to say and to respond to it. Five-year-old children rarely build upon the thoughts of others.

In an open discussion, most children will be eager to contribute. But they often respond to the call to respond alone and not necessarily to the idea of the discussion. In response to a question on what happened in a story, a child might tell about what happened to Grandpop last week, or how her dog likes to jump up when she comes home, or about his new shoes.

It is useful to consider this characteristic behavior when planning situations that enable children to develop the ability to understand a story and to share thoughts about it. It is true that some of the behavior that the children display is developmental. They will all become more able in time. Productive learning situations, however, can be provided that foster abilities in comprehension and language development.

Finding Meaning in a Story

There are some steps you can take to help lead children to think and talk about the meaning of a story. For example, have them restate what happened in a part of a story in their own words, or have several children describe the same incident.

Children at this age are interested in the here and now, not in what happened before or what will happen next. Use questions of what, where, and who. Avoid most questions of how and why. If you do use a how or why question, be certain that the answer is within the realm of the here and now.

The activity "Key Words," on page 21, encourages the children to think about the meanings of key words in a story. This helps them to center their attention on a specific concept. Remember that searching for the meaning of the story is the foremost goal of the discussion. Don't become so involved in delving into the meaning of an individual word that attention is drawn away from understanding the story. The purpose of the activity is to comprehend the story through the meanings of key words.

Developing Comprehension Skills

Kindergarten is a readiness period for reading. The central nontechnical reading skill is comprehension. Comprehension is understanding or finding meaning in what is read. The library media skills program can contribute to building the ability to comprehend.

Several activities included in this chapter involve picture reading. The child looks at an illustration or a series of illustrations in a storybook, thinks about the story that the pictures tell, and shares his or her understanding with other children in the class. While this provides practice in comprehending, it also builds expectations within the child for deriving meaning from books.

Writing Names for Circulation

Circulation procedures usually involve writing the borrower's name in a small space on a book card. At this age, the small muscles needed for this function are not fully developed. Most children find this a challenging task and some are simply not able to do it. Understanding and patience from adults are needed, along with sufficient assistance and practice. Generally, children are strongly motivated to develop this ability and will gradually acquire the skill during the year.

Using Audiovisual Materials

Audiovisual presentations of stories in film, filmstrips, and videotape are especially appealing to children at this age. Most five-year-olds have been watching television daily for several years. The eyes and ears are the first sensory instruments employed for learning and continue to be powerful learning receptors throughout life.

An audiovisual presentation, however, is not an alternative for story reading. Each provides an entirely different experience for the child. Although the content may be the same, the experience is quite different. What is experienced while watching a television program of *The Lorax* by Dr. Seuss is quite different from the experience of listening to the book being read. And both of these experiences are vastly different from that of sitting alone looking at the book. All three are significant experiences for children. None is an exact replica of another.

Each format evokes different images, entails different types of pacing, and calls into play different mental operations. Use all three with the understanding that each provides a different experience for the child.

Summary

The readiness level of the library and information skills instructional program prepares children to use the library media center. They become acquainted with a number of books in the collection, are introduced to the organization of library materials, and learn to follow circulation procedures. The children begin to search for the meanings of stories read to them and to share thoughts about the meanings.

One of the most important outcomes at this level is the development of a positive feeling about using library materials and the library media center in general. This is a delightful, exuberant age when school is a fresh, new experience. Relax and enjoy the children. They will soon look forward to listening to the stories and quickly develop favorites. The library media center can be a wonderful, interesting place for each of them.

READINESS LIBRARY SKILLS CHECKLIST AND ACTIVITIES

The following presents both a sequential checklist of skills for developing young children's readiness to use the library media center and suggested activities for teaching the specific skills on the checklist. Each activity is keyed to one or more of the major skill objectives on the checklist and is ready for your immediate use or adaptation.

The checklist is not meant to be a rigid program of instruction. Rather, it is meant to provide a general framework around which a program may be built. You may find it useful to enter the dates on which a class receives instruction in particular skills. The checklist may also be shared with teachers and others involved in the library and reading programs in your school.

Class _____

I. Location Skills
A. Organization of Materials
1. Knows that materials in the library media center have a specific order
2. Is developing an understanding of own part in keeping materials in order

II. Interpretation Skills
A. Evaluation and Selection Techniques
1. Knows that the library media center has books to borrow and use
2. Knows that many children of all ages use the library media center
3. Can choose a book to borrow with assistance from the library media specialist
4. Can take proper care of the books borrowed
5. Can follow circulation procedures

B. Listening and Viewing Skills
1. Is developing the ability to attend to the sights and sounds of storytelling
2. Is developing ability to respond to what is seen and heard

C. Literature Appreciation
1. Knows there are many storybooks and picture books in the library media center
2. Has some favorite books and main characters

I. LOCATION SKILLS   A. Organization of Materials

WHERE DOES IT LIVE?

This game activity helps children understand that the materials in the library media center have a specific order. It also develops an awareness of their part in keeping materials in order.

Time: 20 minutes

Materials: The collection of easy books in the library media center

NOTE: *This activity is most effective with a small group of 5 to 10 children rather than an entire class. If you attempt it with a class of 20 to 25 children, everyone will not be able to have a turn in the allotted time. In order to hold the attention of the children and to give each an opportunity to participate, it is best to plan this for one small group at a time.*

Activity Directions:

Have the children review alphabetical order by saying the alphabet together. All of the children may not know the alphabet and it is not necessary to teach it to them at this time. Reciting the alphabet together establishes an awareness that letters may be arranged in a certain order like numbers. This is what is important for them to begin to understand.

Explain that the easy section of the library media center is like a street with houses. Ask the children to pretend that each shelf is a house on the street: "The A books live in the A house. The B books live in the B house. Each house has a different letter. The letters on each book tell where the book lives." Point out the shelf labels and the corresponding spine labels on the books.

Give each child a book and ask them to find where the books live. They will probably need your assistance. Let each child take a turn to find the correct shelf for a book while the others look on.

Follow-up: This activity may be repeated at various times throughout the year. The children will gain more and more independence in finding where books belong with additional practice.

II. INTERPRETATION SKILLS   A. Evaluation and Selection Techniques

SURPRISING THINGS

This story activity helps children to understand that a library media center has many kinds of books for them to borrow.

Time: Two 20-minute sessions

Materials: *Tell Me Some More* by Crosby Newell Bonsall.
                New York: Harper and Row, 1961.
                Books from the easy collection of the library media center
Preparation: Select 20 to 30 storybooks—one for each child in the class.
Choose books with lively fantasy stories. Display the books on a low table.
Activity Directions:

Session I—Gather the children around for a story. Read *Tell Me Some
More.* After page 27 ask, "Where are the boys in the story?" Then read to page
32 and ask, "Where is the camel?" After the children have discovered that the
boys are in the library and the camel is in a book, continue reading the story.
Conclude the story and ask, "What kinds of things have you found in books?"
Encourage the children to share some of their thoughts about each question.

Have the children choose books from the display to borrow. Explain that
they will need to look at their books very carefully to find surprising things
that they may tell the other children about the next time they come to the
library media center.

NOTE: *Circulating the books to the children will take more than the
time allotted for this session. You will need to schedule at least an
additional 10 minutes to complete circulation procedures.*

Session II—Have the children sit in a semicircle with the books closed on
their laps. Hold up the book *Tell Me Some More.* Ask the children to recall the
surprising things that the boys found in books in the story from the previous
session. Show the pictures that illustrate these things.

Encourage the children to tell about the surprising things that happened
in their books. Give each child an opportunity to have a turn to share with the
others.

Suggested lively fantasy books for this activity:

Petunia by Roger Duvoisin.
New York: Alfred A. Knopf, 1950.

Lovable Lyle by Bernard Waber.
Boston: Houghton Mifflin, 1969.

The Story of Babar by Jean De Brunhoff.
New York: Random House, 1937.

Katy No Pocket by Emmy Payne.
Boston: Houghton Mifflin, 1964.

Books by Dr Seuss
New York: Random House.

Curious George by H. A. Rey.
Boston: Houghton Mifflin, 1941.

II. INTERPRETATION SKILLS   A. Evaluation and Selection Techniques

MANY HOUSES

This story activity helps children to learn that the library media center has books to borrow and that many children of all ages use the library media center.

Time: 20 minutes

Materials: *Mike Mulligan and His Steam Shovel*
                   by Virginia Lee Burton.
                   Boston: Houghton Mifflin, 1967 and 1939.
                   Mike's House by Julia L. Sauer.
                   New York: The Viking Press, 1954.
                   Storybooks from the easy collection of the library media
                   center

Preparation: Read *Mike Mulligan and His Steam Shovel* during a prior session.

Activity Directions:

Gather the children around for a story. Show the book *Mike Mulligan and His Steam Shovel.* Ask the children to recall the story and choose several children to briefly tell the story. Show the illustrations while the children are recalling the story.

Hold up the book *Mike's House.* Explain that this is a story about a boy who also knew the story about Mike Mulligan. Read the story to the children. Then ask, "Why did the boy call the library Mike's house?" After the children have discussed the answer ask, "Who else might have the library as their house?"

Have available some books that the children are familiar with, such as *Curious George, Babar the King, Harry the Dirty Dog, The Happy Lion.* Show the children each book and and have the children name the main characters and add the word "house" to each suggestion, for example, "Curious George's house."

Suggestions of books for this activity:

Curious George by H. A. Rey.
Boston: Houghton Mifflin, 1941.

Babar the King by Jean De Brunhoff.
New York: Random House, 1937.

Harry the Dirty Dog by Gene Zion.
New York: Harper and Row, 1956.

The Happy Lion by Louise Fatio.
New York: McGraw-Hill, 1954.

Lovable Lyle by Bernard Waber.
Boston: Houghton Mifflin, 1969.

Bread and Jam for Frances by Russell Hoban.
New York: Harper and Row, 1964.

II. INTERPRETATION SKILLS   A. Evaluation and Selection Techniques

CHOOSE YOUR BOOK

This activity enables children to select books with the assistance of the library media specialist. It also provides opportunities for children to become familiar with a variety of storybooks and picture books.

Time: 20-minute sessions

Materials: Books from the easy section of the library media center

Preparation: Select 20 to 30 books, approximately five more than the number of children in the class. Display the books on a low table.

> **NOTE:** *At this age, most children have difficulty selecting a book from the shelves where they can see only the spine of the book. They can choose books more readily if they can see the covers. The table display allows them to recognize familiar books and attracts them to new ones that they haven't seen before.*

Activity Directions:

Have the children form a line and walk slowly around the table displaying the storybooks and picture books. Each child may choose a book and take it to a place on the rug or to a chair to look at it. If the child wants to borrow the book, he or she may go to the circulation desk to sign it out. If the child does not want the book, he or she may return it to the display table and choose another.

Supplementary Activities: This procedure may be followed each time that the entire class comes to the library media center to borrow books.

II. INTERPRETATION SKILLS   A. Evaluation and Selection Techniques

BOOK CARE

This activity helps children to take proper care of books by drawing attention to situations that might damage books.

Time: 20 minutes

Materials: Two pieces of oaktag, 24″ × 36″
                Marking pens of assorted colors

Preparation: Make two posters, one showing things not to do with books and the other showing proper care of books. See the accompanying illustrations.

Activity Directions:

Ask the children if they have books at home. Hold up the chart of things not to do with books. Ask what would happen if they did these things with their books. Point to each picture and have the children explain what would happen to the books in each instance.

Explain that many children read the books in the library media center and that it is important to keep these books in good condition for others to read. Hold up the chart showing the pictures depicting proper care of books. Have the children explain each picture and give examples of times when they did these things.

Follow-up: Hang the charts in a prominent place in the easy section of the library media center.

II. INTERPRETATION SKILLS   A. Evaluation and Selection Techniques

CIRCULATION CARDS

This introduction to circulation procedures also provides practice in following these procedures. Plan to use it prior to the first time the children borrow books from the library media center.

Time: Two 20-minute sessions

Materials: *Rosa-Too-Little* by Sue Felt.
                     New York: Doubleday and Company, 1950.
                     A book card for each child or duplicated replicas of book cards

Activity Directions:

Session I—Gather the class around for a story. Ask them to think of something that they would like to do but are too little to do. Encourage several children to share their experiences. Then tell the children that, in the story, Rosa was too little to do something that she wanted to do. Direct them to listen to find out what it was she wanted to do.

Read *Rosa-Too-Little*. Following the story, have the children tell about how Rosa solved her problem. Establish the concept that she was too little to borrow a book until she learned to write her name on the circulation card.

Session II—Recall the story by asking several children to explain Rosa's problem and how she solved it. Show the corresponding pictures while the children are telling about the story.

Have the children sit at tables. Give each child a book card and a pencil. Explain that to borrow books they must write their names on the book cards and leave them at the circulation desk. Explain that the cards and the books will be stamped with the date when they should return the books to the library media center. Tell the children that they will practice writing their names on the book cards. Demonstrate by writing your name on the first line of a book card and showing it to the class.

Then have the children write their names once on the book cards. Circulate to see that they have their names in the proper place. Assist those needing help. Encourage the children to continue writing their names on the book cards for practice. They may keep the cards for bookmarks.

Variations: You may choose to circulate books to the children before they are able to write their names on the book cards independently. This is often the case where the library media specialist has the assistance of a teacher, clerk, or volunteer. Writing names in the small space provided on book cards is a difficult skill for most five-year-olds. This activity may be used at that time when most of the children are ready to sign the book cards on their own.

II. INTERPRETATION SKILLS   B. Listening and Viewing Skills

FILMSTRIP RESPONSE

This activity helps to develop the ability to attend to the sights and sounds of storytelling through an audiovisual presentation. It gives children experience with responding to what is seen and heard.

Time: 20-minute sessions

Materials: Sound filmstrip—*Curious George* by Margaret and H. A. Rey (New York Times Education Services, 1966)

Books by H. A. Rey in the Curious George series (Boston: Houghton Mifflin)

Activity Directions:

Gather the children around for a story. Explain that they are going to hear a story about Curious George. Hold the book for all of the children to see. Then explain that they are going to see a filmstrip about the story instead of reading the book.

Have the children think about the word *curious*. Ask them to see if they can find times when George was curious while they watch the filmstrip. Show the filmstrip. Afterward have the children tell about the times when George was curious.

Show the display of Curious George books from the collection. Allow time to look through the books and to borrow them.

    NOTE: *There probably won't be enough for all of the children to look at the books at once. Encourage them to take turns.*

    Variation: There are many excellent audiovisual materials available for this level. You may use instructional television programs and films as well as filmstrips. This activity may be repeated throughout the year with a variety of materials. Each time, give the children something to look for during the presentation and have them tell about it afterward.

II. INTERPRETATION SKILLS   C. Literature Appreciation

KEY WORDS

Reading storybooks to children is the principal function of the library media program at the readiness level. This activity introduces them to the variety of materials available for them in the library media center. It also gives them opportunities to develop some favorite books and to become familiar with some main characters that are especially appealing to them.

Time: 20-minute sessions

Materials: Books from the easy collection (see the list of suggested books with key words)

Preparation: Survey the text of the storybook for key words that are central to understanding the story. Choose five or six key words. Too many words will tend to make the story reading choppy, as you will stop to discuss each definition as the word appears in the story.

Activity Directions:

Gather the children around for a story. Read the story with expression and animation, showing the illustrations as you go along. When you come to a key word, stop to ask the children what it means. Encourage the children to participate. When the word has been clearly defined and its relation to the story understood, continue reading the story. Try to limit pauses in reading to the key word discussions. At the end of the story, review the key words and show the corresponding illustrations or concentrate instead on the meaning of the ending of the story.

NOTE: *Children at this age wander in their discussions. They are eager to respond to a call for discussion, but they do not have any compunction to stay with the point being discussed. Ample time for free discussion should be provided. It is also important to provide opportunities for developing the ability to concentrate attention and use language to express a specific point.*

The key word technique tends to center their thoughts on one word and its meaning, which helps them to concentrate their attention on the specific idea in the story. Always relate the meaning of the word to the meaning of the story.

Suggested books with key words:

The Little House by Virginia Lee Burton.
Boston: Houghton Mifflin, 1978.
  different, distance, crowded, noise, shabby, curious

Whose Mouse Are You? by Robert Kraus.
New York: Macmillan Publishing Co., 1970.
  where, far, free, wish, brand new

Drummer Hoff adapted by Barbara Emberly.
Englewood Cliffs, New Jersey: Prentice-Hall, Inc., 1967.
  fired, brought, shot, order

A Baby Sister for Frances by Russell Hoban.
New York: Harper and Row, 1964.
  gravel, cozy, allowance, knapsack, fond, family

II. INTERPRETATION SKILLS   C. Literature Appreciation

PICTURE STORIES

This activity provides practice in deriving meaning from illustrations in storybooks. It prepares children for concentrating on the content of a book in order to find meaning, which is an essential component of reading.

Time: 20-minute sessions

Materials: The storybook and picture book collection of the library media center

Preparation: Arrange a display of storybooks and picture books on a low table. Select books with clear illustrations that tell a simple short story without the necessity of reading the text. Choose stories that are not too complicated or too long. Have one book for each child in the class.

Activity Directions:
Have the children choose books from the display of storybooks and picture books. Ask them to look at the pictures carefully and to think about the story that the pictures tell. Allow five minutes for "reading" the pictures. Encourage the children to be very quiet during this time.

Then ask each child to tell the class the story from the book. They may use the illustrations to show the others what they saw. Continue until all of the children have told their stories.

Follow-up: In order to develop the ability to concentrate attention for finding and sharing meaning from books, repeat this activity throughout the year. Use different storybooks and picture books each time.

Variation: If the children experience difficulty telling the story of an entire book, have them tell about what is happening in one illustration. Gradually they may be able to tell a larger part of the story. After practice and experience with reading pictures, they may tell the complete story of a book.

Suggested storybooks for "reading" pictures.

The Snowy Day by Ezra Jack Keats.
New York: The Viking Press, 1976.

Very Hungry Caterpillar by Eric Carle.
Cleveland, Ohio: Collins World, 1969.

Freight Train by Donald Crews.
New York: Greenwillow, 1978.

Happy Birthday, Sam by Pat Hutchins.
New York: Greenwillow, 1978.

Where the Wild Things Are by Maurice Sendak.
New York: Harper and Row, 1963.

II. FIRST GRADE

Involving Children in Storytelling and Easy-to-Read Books

There are two main activities in the library media center for first graders. One is listening to stories being read and told, and the other is locating and borrowing storybooks and easy-to-read books. These activities are augmented by an introduction to the organization of library materials and an understanding of the function of various parts of books. It is important that children of this age be exposed to a vast and varied assortment of interesting, high-quality books that are read to them and that they begin to read to themselves as well.

This chapter provides:

- A description of first graders' needs in terms of the library program
- A checklist of library skills to be developed at the first level
- Activities for teaching specific skills on the checklist

THE FIRST GRADE PROGRAM

Story Reading and Storytelling

First grade is a transition year in learning to read. The children usually begin as nonreaders and by the end of the year many are reading with some degree of independence.

Before children can read to themselves, they should listen to stories being read because that will develop an interest in books and an awareness of the variety in literature. When children are learning to read, being read to gives them a model of what reading is. It provides experience with the flow of words to form meaning. The children experience the moods and feelings created through reading. They become familiar with the function of punctuation and the use of structure.

Story reading is an opportunity to introduce young children to a wealth of enriching, mind-broadening literature. When considering books to read aloud, choose those with excellent illustrations, such as the Caldecott Award winners. Read a variety of fantasies, humorous stories, realistic stories, and an occasional nonfiction title.

The art of story reading, like that of storytelling, is acquired through experience and practice. It is much more than an expressionless, flat rendering of the text. Story reading is akin to acting, in that it inspires the imagination of the listener. It reaps rewards that make the development of this ability well worth the effort.

Before beginning a story, gather the children into an informal semicircle. Have them all facing you, sitting on a rug or cushions, crosslegged, and fairly close together. You may want to have them sit on low chairs. Position yourself slightly above the children. They should look up at you comfortably without straining to see you.

Relax, smile, and get into the mood of the story. Let this be a time when you put aside all other matters and demands of the library media center. Your reading is a gift that you offer to each child. If you think of it as such, children will grow to treasure it.

Activities Following Reading a Story

The activities that follow listening to a story serve two main purposes. One is to cause the children to understand the meaning of the story and the other is to cause them to relate the meaning to their own experiences. To plan effective follow-up activities it is helpful to understand something about the characteristic behavior and development that children in first grade typically display.

The children are experiencing a period of slow, steady growth, which results in a relatively stable time that is most conducive to learning. The learning that takes place in first grade is highly visible. The child begins as a nonreader and finishes as a reader. Writing and computation skills noticeably improve. Their progress may be readily observed by others and by themselves as well. The children are developing capabilities to express their understanding of the world around them.

Although growth is even at this time, some areas are more advanced than others. The large muscles have more control than the small muscles. The children are not ready for long periods of precise, close work. Although their ability to express ideas and feelings is improving, they still learn most naturally through concrete materials, imaginative play, and imitation of others.

The activities in this section provide three types of follow-up activities for a story: group discussion, dramatization, and drawing. Each type of activity helps children to understand the meaning of a story and to relate the meaning to their own experiences. Each type, also, has unique characteristics and meets children's needs and interests in somewhat different ways. Considering each type of follow-up activity separately provides a fuller understanding of these differences.

Discussion

After listening to a story together, there is nothing more natural than to talk about it together. Group discussion is not only enjoyable, but it brings the experience to either a satisfying culmination or a close. The children will need to be quiet and attentive while listening to the story. Encourage them to save most comments for the discussion following the story. Children at this age want to comment while the story is in progress, but constant interruption causes a loss of continuity and diminishes the impact of the story for the group.

One way to help children to delay their comments and to concentrate on listening for the meaning of the story is to ask a question before you begin the story. Explain that you will talk about the answers together after the story is finished. In this way the attention of the children will be focused during the story. The question should direct them to something that is central to understanding the meaning of the story. At this age children are able to handle only one variable at a time. Ask questions that are simple and direct. Avoid complicated, confusing details that may distract the children from the primary meaning of the story.

After the story, repeat the discussion question and provide ample opportunity for sharing ideas. Six-year-olds all want to be first and need some directions taking turns. To create a relaxed yet concentrated environment for listening and expressing thoughts to one another, it is helpful to establish two simple ground rules.

1. Only one person speaks at a time.
2. Everyone listens to the speaker.

Give each child who wishes to speak a turn. Children will be more willing to save their comments until after the story and to listen to the comments of others if they are assured of being given a hearing during each discussion.

Dramatization

Dramatization following a story is especially suited to the needs and interests of first graders. Six-year-olds are very active and learn through imaginative play and imitation of others, sometimes referred to as role playing. They have not perfected their skills in reading, writing, and talking sufficiently to fully express their ideas. They need opportunities to actively use their bodies to express thoughts.

The dramatization activities on pages 37 and 40 may be enlarged upon. When planning dramatization activities for first graders, keep instructions clear and simple. Six-year-olds can be aggressive and uncooperative. A complicated, confusing situation will often draw these traits to the fore.

Children of this age want to be first, but they want to be liked as well. They will generally participate cooperatively in a group dramatization if they know exactly what is expected of them. Establish clear, concise patterns for them to follow. They haven't as yet had sufficient experience to have formed habits for positive group participation. They will need definite instructions on how to proceed.

A simple, well-planned dramatization activity produces delightful results. Encourage and enjoy the spontaneous, uninhibited creativity of children of this age.

Drawing

A third kind of activity to use after a story is drawing. An example of this is the activity "Real Toys," on page 42. As previously mentioned, six-year-olds are not yet able to express themselves through writing. Drawing is a very natural way of expressing ideas and thoughts at this age. Often, drawing abilities that are apparent at six and earlier disappear or go underground as language and writing skills increase in older children.

Drawing is not merely decorative; it is a way of expressing something that cannot be expressed in any other way. Drawing in response to a question about the meaning of a story is an excellent way for each child to express individually his or her own understanding. In this way, each child relates the story to the experiences of his or her own unique background. Have the children explain their drawings to each other for a rich sharing experience.

Using Audiovisual Materials

There are many excellent audiovisual materials of stories available for first graders in the form of television, films, and filmstrips. When you show these to the children, do so with the understanding that they are not alternatives to reading the story, but rather a mode that provides an entirely different experience for the children.

Since they are watching many hours of television, it is extremely important that children have opportunities to talk about the meaning of what they have viewed. For them to understand and to begin to evaluate this vast bombardment of random information and entertainment, they need to search for meaning in what they view and to relate its meaning to their own experiences. These are essential skills in our lives that are often left underdeveloped without the aid of instruction. Learning situations in which children talk about what they are viewing are an important part of library and information skills instruction.

Reading Comprehension

The main task at school for the first grader is learning to read. Reading instruction continues throughout elementary school, but the initial, concentrated effort is made in the first grade.

There are two major aspects of reading: word attack and comprehension. While library media specialists do not teach word attack skills, they are very much involved in comprehension. Reading comprehension is understanding the meaning of what is read. The activities previously described for following a story help increase comprehension abilities. Discussion, dramatization, and drawing help children to develop the ability to find meaning in a story. These activities also build expectations within children that books are meaningful and comprehensible.

Easy-to-Read Books

As reading skills develop, children need a variety of books and magazines to read. Provide an abundant collection of easy-to read books, organized and located so that the children can browse freely. You might want to separate these books from the easy collection and place them together on low shelves in an area where the children can gather on the floor or on cushions. Here they can sample a variety of these books and develop some favorites. There are many easy-to-read books on the market. A list of titles is included in the activity entitled "Individual Reading," on page 35.

Some children will move beyond the easy-to-read books before the end of first grade. Be alert for these readers and guide them toward books in the collection that are a bit more difficult and are still of interest to six-year-olds. It is difficult for children to choose books if only the spine of the book is showing. They will need some assistance in selecting books that they can read and understand.

When children are first learning to read, it is time to put highly appealing books into their hands. Don't miss this golden opportunity to capture their excitement and enthusiasm over their new-found skill and to channel it toward a deep-seated interest in and enjoyment of books. Encourage early independent reading habits.

The Nonfiction Collection

First graders often ask for books on specific topics which are part of the nonfiction collection of the library media center. Use this opportunity to introduce the nonfiction collection and the concept that there is subject access to library media center materials. First graders will need your help to locate books that are appropriate for them, books that they can read or those in which they can understand at least the pictures. Occasionally a child will display a consistent interest in a certain subject, such as dinosaurs, ballet, or dogs. After being shown the appropriate section, the child will return repeatedly on his or her own to find such books.

Organization of Materials

While the children are browsing, choosing, and borrowing books, they are gradually developing an understanding that library media center materials are in a certain order and that this order makes it possible to find specific materials. They can learn that they have a part in keeping this order. Markers made of strips of colored construction paper may be used by the children to indicate the place of a book on the shelf while they look at it. The children can begin to understand that the library media center is their place, which they share with the other children in the school. It is not "owned" by the library media specialist. The materials are for them to use, but the responsibility of caring for the materials and keeping the order is shared by them also.

Parts of a Book

While you are introducing a book that you are going to read to the children, point out the various parts of the book and explain their functions. Children should develop the concept that all books are organized in the same basic way. This understanding will help them when they begin to read independently. For example, knowing that all books have a title page, which tells who wrote, printed, and distributed the book, prevents confusion when first opening a book. If, instead, they think that a book only contains a story, the title page is a strange beginning indeed. If children understand the purpose of the title page, it becomes a useful orientation to the book.

Summary

In the first grade, children become familiar with a variety of different kinds of books that are read to them or that they look at on their own. After listening to a story, they become involved in an activity that draws out the meaning for them. These activities of discussion, dramatization, and drawing, in addition to more individual activities of browsing, choosing, and borrowing, make the library media center a lively place for first graders. They find it is a place to share ideas and feelings about what is seen and heard as well as a place to listen and read quietly.

FIRST GRADE LIBRARY SKILLS CHECKLIST AND ACTIVITIES

The following presents a sequential checklist of library and information skills to be developed at the first grade level and a number of suggested activities for teaching specific skills. Each activity is keyed to one or more of the major skill objectives on the checklist and includes detailed directions for its use.

Library Skills Checklist
FIRST GRADE

Class _____

I. Location Skills
A. Card Catalog
1. Knows that the materials in the library media center have a specific arrangement
2. Understands own part in keeping materials in order

B. Fiction and Nonfiction
1. Has initial understanding of the difference between fiction and nonfiction materials
2. Has used both fiction and nonfiction materials

C. Periodicals
1. Knows that the library media center has materials other than books
2. Is familiar with magazines that are of interest

D. Audiovisual Materials and Equipment
1. Knows that the library media center has materials other than books
2. Can find meaning in an audiovisual presentation

II. Interpretation Skills
A. Evaluation and Selection Techniques
1. Can select books of interest to him/her
2. Can select books that he/she can read

B. Parts of a Book
1. Can identify the cover, both front and back
2. Can identify the spine and spine label
3. Can identify the title page
4. Can identify the title, author, and illustrator

C. Listening and Viewing Skills
1. Is able to attend to the sights and sounds of storytelling
2. Can participate in discussion following a story

D. Literature Appreciation
1. Knows that a variety of books are available
2. Can draw the point of the story into own experience

I. LOCATION SKILLS   A. Card Catalog

FIND THE SHELF

This activity leads the children to an understanding that the materials in the library media center have a specific arrangement.

Time: 30 minutes

Materials: $3'' \times 5''$ cards, unlined

   Marking pens

Preparation: Make a set of cards with a letter of the alphabet on each one.

Activity Directions:

Show the spine labels on the books in the easy section of the library media center collection to the children. Explain that the letters on the labels indicate the shelf on which the book belongs: "All of the A books are on the A shelf and the B books are on the B shelf."

Choose two children to work as partners. Give them one of the cards with a letter printed on it. Have the partners find the corresponding shelf label and choose any book by an author whose name starts with the letter. Remind them to check the spine label of the books to help them find the book more easily. Have the children insert a marker in the place where they found the book. Help the children read the name of the author and the call number. Then have the partners return the book to its proper place. Allow all of the children to have a turn.

NOTE: *At this age, the activity alone is sufficient to hold interest. It is not necessary to build competition into the game.*

Variation: As the children become proficient in locating the books, you may wish to have them find books by the first three letters of the author's last name. They may also work individually instead of remaining with partners.

I. LOCATION SKILLS   B. Fiction and Nonfiction

NONFICTION BOOKS

Although first graders will not have a full understanding of the difference between fiction and nonfiction, they can begin to see that materials are available with information on various topics. The following activity is planned to introduce them to nonfiction books.

Time: 30 minutes

Materials: *Panda* by Susan Bonners.

   New York: Delacorte Press, 1978.

Activity Directions:

Explain that in a library all of the books are either fiction or nonfiction: "The stories that we have been reading together are fiction. They are made up by someone using imagination and do not necessarily tell real facts. Today we are going to read a nonfiction book." Hold the book up and open to some of the pages. Show several illustrations and say, "Can you tell how this book is different from the other books we have read together?" Give the children an opportunity to express their ideas: "Listen while I read the book to find out how this book is different."

Read the book and show the illustrations. Point out that, although the illustrations are drawings, they are realistic and resemble photographs. Allow the children to absorb some of the facts and information in the book by stopping occasionally to reflect together on a point of interest. After reading the book have the children discuss the difference between this nonfiction book and fiction books with which they are familiar. Develop the concept that nonfiction contains facts and information about real things or topics.

Follow-up: Repeat this lesson several times using other nonfiction books. The following books are recommended for this activity:

Possum Baby by Berniece Freschet.
New York: G. P. Putnam and Son, 1978.

How to Be a Nature Detective by Millicent Selsam.
New York: Harper and Row, 1966.

I. LOCATION SKILLS   C. Periodicals

CHILDREN'S MAGAZINES

This activity provides an opportunity for the children to know that the library media center has materials other than books. It also enables them to become familiar with magazines that are of interest to them.

Time: 30 minutes
Materials: Magazines from the periodical collection on the primary level, such as *Children's Playmate, Humpty Dumpty, Jack and Jill,* and *Highlights for Children*
Preparation: Prepare a display of back issues of primary magazines from the library media center collection. Spread the magazines out on a low table.
Activity Directions:
Choose the latest issue of each magazine. Show and discuss the cover illustration. Ask the children why they think that the illustration was chosen for this month. Turn to the table of contents and show the children that there are different kinds of things in the magazine. Read the items listed in the table of contents to show that there are stories, things to do, articles with information on real topics, contributions by readers, poems, songs, and jokes and riddles.

Select one of the feature columns in the magazine, such as jokes and riddles, and briefly do the activity with the children. If time allows, read a short story from one of the magazines.

Have the children choose a magazine from the display of back issues. Allow 10 minutes for the children to read their magazines. Then have each child tell about something in the magazine that he or she found interesting.

Follow-up: You may wish to circulate the magazines in place of a book or in addition to books.

Variation: This activity may be divided into two sessions. Use the first session to introduce the magazines and the second to have the children read and share what they found.

I. LOCATION SKILLS   D. Audiovisual Materials and Equipment

BROKEN PROMISES

This activity acquaints children with materials other than books in the library media center. It also provides an opportunity to talk about the meaning of what is seen and heard in an audiovisual presentation.

Time: 30 minutes

Materials: *Gather 'Round* (Falls Church, Virginia: ITV Co-op)

Gather 'Round is a series of 16 storytelling programs available on public television, produced by Children's Television International, Skyline Center Suite 1207, 5205 Leesburg Pike, Falls Church, Virginia 22401.

The Princess and the Pea
The Brementown Musicians
Beauty and the Beast
Puss in Boots
Rapunzel
Kalulu and the Leopard
The Fisherman and His Wife
The Pied Piper of Hamlin
The Frog Prince
The Golden Goose
The Shoemaker and the Elves
The Ugly Duckling
Cinderella
The Brothers and the Singing Toad
The Theft of Fire
Brother Rabbit's Astonishing Prank

The story used in the following activity is *The Frog Prince.*

Activity Directions:

Gather the children for a story. Ask if they have ever made a promise. Have several children tell about their promises. Then ask if they have ever made a promise that they had trouble keeping. Encourage the children to share their experiences. Explain that in the story the princess had trouble keeping her promises. Have the children look for broken promises while they are viewing the television story. Show the program, which lasts 15 minutes. After the television story, give the children an opportunity to talk about the princess's promises and why she couldn't keep them.

Variations: This activity may be repeated throughout the year. There are a variety of high-quality audiovisual materials available on television as well as films and filmstrips from which to choose. Before showing an audiovisual presentation, always give the children something to look for during the viewing. After the presentation, encourage them to talk about what they saw and heard.

NOTE: *Most children watch many hours of television each day. It is important for them to have opportunities to talk about the meaning of what they view and to relate the meaning to their own experiences.*

II. INTERPRETATION SKILLS   A. Evaluation and Selection Techniques

INDIVIDUAL READING

This activity develops the abilities of children to select books that interest them and that they can read by themselves. It should be used after the children have had several months of reading instruction and are able to read limited, simple vocabulary books.

Time: 30 minutes

Materials: Easy-to-read books such as those suggested below

Preparation: Select approximately 10 easy-to-read books to display in the easy section of the library media center.

NOTE: *The easy-to-read books may be separated from the rest of the easy collection and shelved together permanently to enable first graders to find these books independently.*

Activity Directions:
Explain that there are some books written especially for new readers. Describe each book on display by reading the title and the author and telling a little about the story, showing one or two of the illustrations.

Read one chapter of *Owl at Home*, by Arnold Lobel. (Any easy-to-read book with chapters may be substituted.) Explain that this book has more than one story with the same characters: "Each story is a separate chapter with its own title. All of the chapters are listed in the table of contents with the beginning page numbers."

Have each child choose an easy-to-read book from those on display or others in the collection. Allow 5 to 10 minutes for individual silent reading. Circulate among the children to give help with any words that they can't read. Encourage each child to borrow a book that he or she can read independently.

Follow-up: This activity may be repeated several times throughout the year using books of increasing difficulty.

Here are some suggested books to use for this activity:

The Strange Disappearance of Arthur Cluck by Nathaniel Benchley.
New York: Harper and Row, 1967.

Bears' Picnic by Stanley and Janice Berenstain.
New York: Random House, 1966.

Big Honey Hunt by Stanley and Janice Berenstain.
New York: Random House, 1962.

Grizzwold by Syd Hoff.
New York: Harper and Row, 1963.

Stanley by Syd Hoff.
New York: Harper and Row, 1962.

Frog and Toad All Year by Arnold Lobel.
New York: Harper and Row, 1976.

Grasshopper on the Road by Arnold Lobel.
New York: Harper and Row, 1978.

Owl at Home by Arnold Lobel.
New York: Harper and Row, 1975.

Little Bear by Else Holmelund Minarik.
New York: Harper and Row, 1957.

Amelia Bedelia by Peggy Parish.
New York: Harper and Row, 1963.

Teach Us, Amelia Bedelia by Peggy Parish.
New York: Greenwillow, 1977.

Green Eggs and Ham by Dr. Seuss.
New York: Random House, 1960.

II. INTERPRETATION SKILLS   B. Parts of a Book

GUESS WHAT PART

This review game gives children practice in identifying the various parts of a book: cover, spine and spine label, title page, title, author, and illustrator.

Time: 20 to 30 minutes

Preparation: At the beginning of storytelling or reading for 5 to 10 sessions, introduce each part of a book until the children are acquainted with all of the seven parts identified above.

Activity Directions:

List the seven parts of a book on a chart or chalkboard. Start the game by describing one of the parts of a book and asking the children to guess what it is.

For example, say, "I am on the outside of the book. I am usually hard and protect the pages of the book. What am I?" The child who guesses correctly may come forward to describe another part of a book for the children to guess. Continue until all parts have been described at least once. The children may repeat parts of books already described by adding some new trait not previously mentioned.

Follow-up: This review game may be repeated once or twice. After several sessions, interest usually wanes somewhat because of the limited parts of a book to be described.

II. INTERPRETATION SKILLS   **C. Listening and Viewing Skills**

STORY PUPPET SHOW

This dramatization encourages children to attend to the sights and sounds of storytelling in order to participate in the puppet show following the story. It provides opportunities for summarizing, paraphrasing, and extending a story.

Time: Five 30-minute sessions

NOTE: *This is a multisession activity. You will need to provide at least five 30-minute sessions in succession.*

Materials: *The Hole in the Dike* by Norma Green.
            New York: Thomas Y. Crowell, 1975.
            Small paper bags, $5'' \times 3'' \times 10''$, one for each child
            Construction paper in assorted colors
            Scissors
            Paste
            Crayons
            Oaktag, $24'' \times 36''$, two pieces

Activity Directions:

Session I—Read the story to the class. Have them discuss the following question: "Have you ever known someone very young who did a very brave and important act?" Encourage the children to share experiences.

Session II—Gather the children around to plan a puppet show of the story. Recall the story by having several children summarize the story for the others. Show the illustrations and point out the characters, the background, and the props needed. Choose four to six children to make the background and props. Then select children for the following characters: four boys, four girls, six women, and six men.

NOTE: *These numbers are for a class of approximately 24 to 26 children. You may adjust according to the number of children in the class with which you are working.*

Session III—Have the children sit at tables. Demonstrate how to make the three types of hats, one for the men, one for the boys, and one for the women and girls. Draw the three types of hats on the chalkboard (see illustration).

Give each child a paper bag and a piece of colored paper for the hats—white for the girls and women, blue for the boys, and assorted bright colors for the men. Have the children draw the hats, cut them out, and paste them to the closed end of the paper bag. The children may then complete the puppets by drawing faces and clothing with crayon. Encourage them to be creative and use their own ideas.

Have the children making the background design two scenes, one with a windmill, cottage, and tulips, and another with water, a boat, the dike and a road below (see illustration). They will also need to make the following props: a bicycle, a stone, a stick, and a truck.

Sessions IV and V—Divide the class into two groups. Each group should have a full set of characters, two boys, two girls, three women, and three men. Assign two children to hold the background and one to be in charge of props for each group. Have the groups meet for a planning session to decide who will play each character. Assist the groups where needed. Allow 10 minutes for planning.

One group may play the puppet show while the other group is the audience. You may narrate the story or choose a child to read the story while the players perform the dramatization.

Follow-up: The puppet show may be given for other classes.

Variation: Puppet shows may be used to dramatize other stories. Choose books with approximately 10 characters, a simple story line, and those that have characters that lend themselves to simple puppet making.

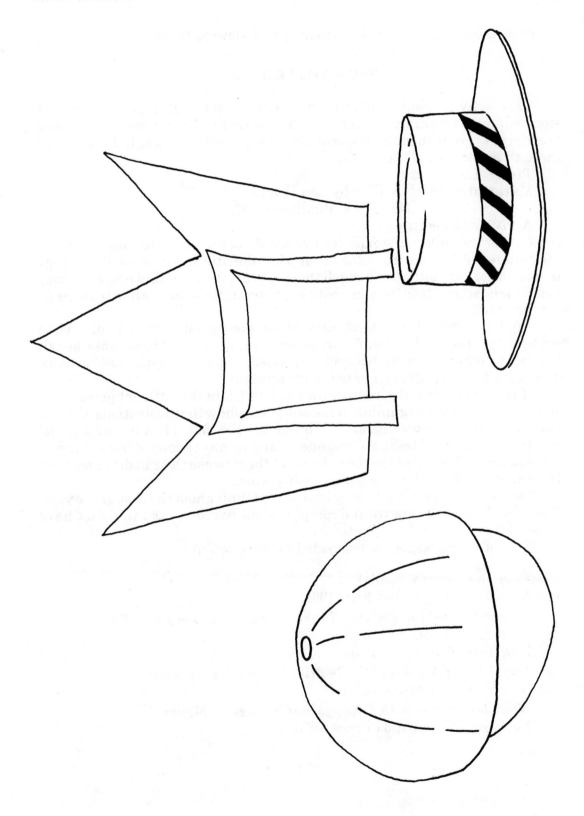

II. INTERPRETATION SKILLS   C. Listening and Viewing Skills

SHOW THE FEELINGS

This activity helps children to attend to the sights and sounds of storytelling and reading in order to participate in the dramatization following the story. It gives them an opportunity to express the meaning of the story through action as well as words.

Time: 30 minutes

Materials: *Fish Is Fish* by Leo Lionni.
                        New York: Pantheon, 1970.

Activity Directions:

Gather the children around for a story. Read the title of the story and ask the children if they have an idea about what the title might mean. Encourage them to offer suggestions. Then tell them to see if they can find out while they listen to the story. Read the story with expression, showing the illustrations as you proceed.

After the story is finished, talk about the meaning of the title. Then explain that the fish had different feelings in the story: "Sometimes he felt happy. At other times he felt sad, surprised, lonely, disappointed, jealous, determined, frightened, contented, and thankful."

Have the children dramatize how the fish felt in the different parts of the story. Start with the beginning of the story and show the illustrations. Choose one child to act the way he or she thinks the fish felt. Then have all of the children display that feeling. Continue until they have depicted the feelings of the fish on each page of the book. Remind them to use their bodies and their faces to show the feeling instead of using words.

Variation: This activity may be repeated throughout the first grade year. Have the children dramatize and role play some part of a story that they have listened to.

The following books are suggested for this activity.

Pierre by Maurice Sendak.
New York: Harper and Row, 1962.

Alexander and the Terrible, Horrible, No Good, Very Bad Day
by Judith Viorst.
New York: Atheneum, 1976.

May I Bring A Friend? by Beatrice Schenk De Regniers.
New York: Atheneum, 1974.

What Do You Do with a Kangaroo? by Mercer Mayer.
New York: Four Winds Press, 1973.

II. INTERPRETATION SKILLS   C. Listening and Viewing Skills

SHARING EXPERIENCES

This group activity develops children's abilities to attend to the sights and sounds of storytelling. It gives each child the chance to participate in a discussion related to the story and to draw the point of the story into his or her own experience.

Time: 30 minutes

Materials: *Mushroom in the Rain* by Mirra Ginsburg.
New York: Macmillan Publishing Company, 1974.

Activity Directions:

Prior to reading the story, ask the children to think of a time when they had something that they thought they had enough of only for themselves, but when they shared it there was enough for others too. Let the children share their experiences by using these rules: Only one person speaks at a time, and everyone listens to the speaker.

Next, read the story and show the pictures. To maximize concentration on the story, encourage the children to save most comments for a discussion following the story.

At the conclusion of the story, ask the children if they were surprised by the ending: "Did you ever have something happen to you that didn't end the way that you expected? Tell us about how you were surprised."

Continue the discussion until all children have had at least one turn to share experiences.

Follow-up: You can repeat this technique with other books by developing a question to direct children's attention to certain aspects of the story before the story begins and another question to direct discussion at the conclusion.

NOTE: *Discussion should be redirected toward the question whenever the children stray from the point under consideration.*

II. INTERPRETATION SKILLS   D. Literature Appreciation

WHAT REALLY HAPPENED?

This activity helps children to draw the point of a story into their own experience. It also acquaints them with a variety of books in the library media center collection.

Time: 30 minutes

Materials: *Mitten* by Alvin Tresselt.
New York: Lothrop, Lee V. Shepard Co., 1964.

Activity Directions:

Before reading the story, tell the children to listen very carefully to see if they think this is what really happened. Read the story with expression, showing the illustrations as you proceed.

After the story, ask the children if they know who was telling the story. Then explain that when the grandfather was a little boy he dropped his mitten. When he returned, he found that it was ripped. Show the corresponding illustrations. Have the children tell what they think happened to the mitten. Encourage them to use their imagination to tell a story of what might have happened. Provide an opportunity for all of the children who want to share their ideas to have a turn.

Variation: This activity may be used with other stories. Before you read the story, give the children something to look for during the story. After the story, have the children talk about their ideas.

Other books to use for this activity are:

Keep Your Mouth Closed, Dear by Aliki,
New York: Dial Press, 1966.

Be Nice to Spiders by Margaret Bloy Graham.
New York: Harper and Row, 1967.

Alexander and the Windup Mouse by Leo Lionni.
New York: Pantheon, 1969,

The Biggest House in the World by Leo Lionni.
New York: Pantheon, 1968.

Swimmy by Leo Lionni.
New York: Pantheon, 1963.

II. INTERPRETATION SKILLS   D. Literature Appreciation

"REAL" TOYS

This activity gives the children an opportunity to draw the point of the story into their own experience.

Time: 30 to 45 minutes

Materials: *The Velveteen Rabbit* by Margery Williams.
New York: Doubleday and Company, 1958;
Avon (paperback), 1975
Drawing paper for each child
Crayons

Activity Directions:

Gather the children around for a story. Read the first section of the book, stopping at page 24. Ask the children if they have ever had a toy that became "real." Give several children the opportunity to talk about their favorite toys both at the present time and at a time when they were younger.

Have the children sit at tables. Pass around paper and crayons. Ask them to draw the toy they liked so much that it became more than just a toy; it became "real." After they have finished their drawings, have each show the class and tell about their "real" toys.

Follow-up: You may continue reading the story during another session, or you may suggest that the children take the book home to finish the story.

Bulletin Board or Showcase Display: Ask the children to lend their "real" toys to the library media center for a week. They will usually be willing to part with the toys for a short time. Display them with the pictures and place the book, *The Velveteen Rabbit,* in the display. Make a caption: "Our Real Toys. Do You Remember Yours?" Older children enjoy reminiscing about their old toys, too.

III. SECOND GRADE

Helping Children Toward Independent Reading

The library media center program for second grade focuses on listening to stories being read or told and selecting books to borrow. After listening to stories, the children participate in activities that help them to understand the meaning of the story and to recall, summarize, and paraphrase what they have heard and seen. As the children's reading skills develop, it is essential that they have a variety of books to read independently. If they leave second grade knowing that the library media center has interesting books that they can read to themselves, you have accomplished your major goal.

This chapter provides:

- A description of second graders' needs in terms of the library program
- A checklist of library skills to be developed at the second level
- Activities for teaching specific skills

THE SECOND GRADE PROGRAM

When reading books to second graders, follow much the same pattern as with first graders. Gather the children in an informal semicircle facing you. Have them sit crosslegged or on low chairs and position yourself slightly above them. By now, they are familiar with this routine and will generally settle down quickly and be ready to listen to the story with a minimum of direction.

Selecting Stories to Read

Select stories with absorbing plots and stories in which the children can identify with the feelings of the characters. Seven-year-old children have a longer attention span and can concentrate on more subtle details. They have a lively imagination, an outrageous sense of humor, and a keen sense of the right and wrong way of doing things. Choose humorous stories, scary stories, stories with surprise endings and subtle twists. Read books that provide rich listening experiences that are lively and fun.

You might wish to select books that center around one theme or one type of literature. For example, folk tales and fairy tales are especially appealing to second graders. These stories are available in an abundance of high-quality materials. Some suggested titles are included with the activities in this chapter.

Illustrations

A variety of highly skillful artists illustrate children's books. These illustrations enhance the story-reading experience that you provide for second graders. Describe the various media in which the artists have worked to create the illustrations. The children will be interested to know that many techniques are used. Draw attention to the more subtle points of the illustrations. Note the way the illustrations express feelings of amusement or sadness or pain or joy. The children can appreciate these details, which enrich the way the story is experienced. Avoid becoming so involved in details, however, that the central point of the story is clouded.

Audiovisual Materials

There are excellent audiovisual materials available for second grade children. Provide opportunities for them to view stories presented on television, film, or filmstrips and to express the meaning of what they see.

Reading stories that the children have seen in an audiovisual presentation or on television makes the children aware of the contrast in the way that they experience the story through each mode. In this way, they begin to understand that what they view on television and what they read in books cannot replace each other. Each medium affects his or her thinking differently. In our culture, we learn from many kinds of media.

The activities that follow an audiovisual presentation, like those following a story, give the children opportunities to express the meaning of what they have viewed by relating it to their own background experiences. In this way, they learn techniques to understand more fully what they view and begin to analyze and evaluate the role of television and other media in their lives.

Follow-up Activities

Three types of activities follow listening to a story: discussion, dramatization, and drawing. These same three D's were used in first grade to enable children to understand and express the meaning of a story. In second grade, these activities help children to begin to analyze and evaluate what they see and hear. They provide opportunities for recalling, summarizing, and paraphrasing.

Recalling

Recalling is thinking back on what was seen and heard to remember the events and mood of a story or the information in nonfiction materials. The activities in this section call for remembering immediately following a story as well as recalling a story heard during a previous session. The children begin to become aware of the difference between short-term and long-term memory abilities. Have the children recall parts of stories as well as whole stories. Ask them to recall sequences of happenings, and to single out specific events in a story.

The role of memory in thinking and learning is substantial. We recall things by thinking of certain aspects that provide cues for our memory. These cues lead to fuller, more complete recall of the thing. The cue may be an image, a word, or a feeling. These activities help to develop recall abilities by drawing attention to certain aspects of stories, which later become cues to aid remembering.

Recalling is a result of effective listening. Children need not only to listen *to* something, but also to listen *for* something. Asking children to listen in order to answer a question aids recall considerably.

Summarizing

Summarizing is telling what happened in a capsulized way. The children may be asked to summarize the events of what happened in a story. This is a quick telling of what happened at the beginning, in the middle, and at the end. The feeling of the characters may also be summarized, as well as the overall meaning or main point of the story.

Summarizing enables children to think of the story all at once. It brings the story into some manageable form for them to analyze and evaluate. It requires that they cut away some of the more insignificant points to concentrate on the central theme of the story.

This is an extremely difficult task for children. They want to tell all, to leave out nothing. They often become involved in details and miss the main idea. Summarizing is a crucial skill used in thinking and learning.

The follow-up activities in this section help children to summarize by putting them into situations in which they are forced to summarize in order to accomplish the task. In tasks of discussion, dramatization, and drawing that

are enjoyable and meaningful for the children, the incentive to summarize is
built into the activity.

Paraphrasing

Paraphrasing is telling something in one's own words. It is extremely
important that the children have opportunities to repeat a story in the way
that they would say it. When asked to show his surprise at finding a treasure,
one second grader pantomimed walking along, seeing something, bending
down to examine it, and then exclaimed, "Mama mia!" This delightfully
descriptive paraphrasing was brought from the child's experience.

Paraphrasing draws on the abilities to recall and to summarize to a
culmination and a close. The child first recalls what is seen and heard, then
summarizes or thinks it through to capsulize the experience for telling, and
then paraphrases or shares the account in his or her own manner of speaking.
Paraphrasing personalizes the telling and is a highly individual activity. It is
the step prior to extending, which is taking the telling beyond what is recalled
to create some new idea or thought. Extending is introduced in second grade
and will be developed in later grades.

The Three D's to Follow a Story

Seven-year-old children alternate between very active and more quiet
behavior. The quiet activity of listening to a story followed by an activity
calling for active participation in discussion, dramatization, or drawing is
especially suited to children at this age. Discussion, dramatization, and
drawing follow stories in second grade, as well as in first grade, but in the
second grade these activities require somewhat more refined abilities.

Discussion

Children at seven are talkative, open, and ready to communicate. When
guiding discussions with second graders, you may find it helpful to set up some
basic rules. To the two rules that were introduced in first grade discussion, a
third may be added:

1. Only one person speaks at a time.
2. Everyone listens to the speaker.
3. Responses to discussion questions should be relevant and to the
   point.

Keeping responses limited to the point being discussed is difficult for
second graders. They often want to share extraneous experiences. If the
children are to derive meaning from the discussion, a gentle steering back on
the track is necessary.

A productive discussion depends on understandable, thought-provoking
questions. The questions should direct attention to the main point of the story.
Develop questions that generate lively analysis. Use open questions without
set answers, ones that will stimulate children to express ideas that you are

truly interested to hear. For example, following a folk tale or fairy tale, you might ask, "Was the main character lucky or clever?"

In a discussion, encourage the children to use their own ideas and language and to draw examples from their experiences. Accept differences of opinion. It is not necessary or desirable to reach a consensus at the end of every discussion.

Discussions with second grade children are spontaneous, lively affairs, with many opinions and comments being expressed in rapid succession. Keep the discussions relatively short, 5 to 10 minutes, to maintain the enthusiasm and interest of the children.

Dramatization

Seven-year-old children learn through role playing and imitating others. Although their skills in reading and writing are constantly improving, they need opportunities to express ideas through action. They respond naturally to simple dramatization situations where they can recall, summarize, and paraphrase through acting out what they have seen and heard.

Dramatization helps children to understand the story through opportunities to feel or act like the characters. They find meaning in a story by relating it to their own background experience. Dramatization helps children to feel and act out things they haven't experienced by relating these things to an experience they have had that was similar or that evoked the same feeling. For example, say to the children, "The girl in the story was angry. Have you ever been angry? Show how you think she felt." In this way the children can more fully understand what is being read.

Children of this age are active, talkative, and competitive. To perform satisfying dramatizations in which they can all participate, they will need a clear understanding of what is expected of them and how to proceed. Seven-year-olds tend to be sensitive to the feelings and attitudes of both peers and adults and are quite cooperative in group activities if they are given a simple pattern to follow.

Explain to the children that while one child or group of children is performing, the rest are the audience. The audience watches and reacts, but does not call out instructions or cues. If the players need assistance to recall or if they need advice on acting, they may ask the audience for help. The other children may then raise their hands and wait to be chosen to share their ideas. The call for assistance is always initiated by the player, never by the audience. In this way, the players may work through their action without inhibiting, and sometimes intimidating, distractions. The children in the audience, of course, will each have a turn to be a player.

Drawing

Drawing is very closely related to writing at this age. When you ask children to write about something, they will often ask if they can draw a picture instead of, or in addition to, the writing.

Drawing is a very natural means of communication at this age. A means of communication is a way of saying something or expressing something. Children generally draw for themselves, however, and not necessarily to communicate to another person. At this age, children seldom tell you that they can't draw something. They usually just make it as well as they can and are not overly concerned about how real or perfect their drawing is.

When you ask the children to draw in response to a story, have them share their drawings with the other children. Encourage them to talk about their drawings and explain the ideas that they have expressed in the drawings. This combines the use of pictures and words to express ideas, which is the same combination that they come in contact with in books. In this way the children are learning to express ideas in different modes. They will continue to use these ways of expressing ideas and feelings in reading and writing.

Reading

As reading abilities of second graders improve, it remains important that they have opportunities to scan and to choose from a quantity of interesting books that they are able to read. After they have developed initial decoding skills, reading for meaning enables them to make leaps in comprehension and vocabulary competencies.

Poor motivation is one of the major causes of reading problems. When children feel that books have nothing interesting to offer to them, there is little incentive to read independently. On the other hand, when they are fascinated with a story or a topic and are pressing forward to understand the meaning of what they are reading, their reading ability often increases by leaps and bounds.

As a library media specialist, you are in the unique position of knowing the children as well as the library media center collection. You can often put the two together at the magic moment that captures the child's enthusiasm for reading.

The library media center program and the instructional reading program can be dovetailed into a mutual support system. The materials that are provided for second graders in the library media center to read independently or to be read to them can be effectively related to the reading instruction provided in the classroom. This is not an easy task and can only be accomplished by joint planning and continuing conversations between the teacher and the library media specialist. The library media specialist needs to know something about the reading ability of individual children. The teacher needs to know something about the books that are available for the children to read. At this age, the children can derive great pleasure and satisfaction from their newly acquired ability to read books independently. It is well worth the time and effort involved to form ties between reading instruction and the library media center program.

Locating Books for Independent Reading

By second grade, children are very familiar with the easy collection and can locate favorites with little assistance. Encourage them to help each other to locate interesting books and to recommend books that they have enjoyed.

Locating books to read from the fiction collection is more difficult for second graders. Many of the books are intended for older children and will be beyond their reading ability and outside of their realm of experience and interest. The children will need your guidance to find fiction books that are right for them. Second grade classes often develop favorite books that they pass from one child to another. Some of the books by Beverly Cleary and those by Carolyn Haywood are longtime favorites. Once the children are introduced to an author whose books they enjoy reading, they often return to sample other titles by the same person.

At this age many children increasingly turn their attention to specific topics in nonfiction materials. When they understand that the books are shelved together by the subject, they often ask where the books are that contain information on a certain topic, such as soccer, gymnastics, care for pets, or bike riding. If the topic is of continuing interest, they often remember where the section is located and return on their own. The activity "My Collection," on page 56, acquaints the children with the location of books on their hobbies and personal interests.

Second grade children will need guidance to find nonfiction books that they are able to read. Sometimes they can understand extensively illustrated materials, although they cannot read the text. You will need to help them choose nonfiction books that they can learn from and enjoy.

Reference

Second grade children can use children's encyclopedias, such as *Childcraft*, that have general information in simple reading vocabulary. In a discussion in the second grade classroom, a question might arise that requires further information and facts in order to be fully answered. This is an opportune time for one child or a small group of children to go to the library media center to use an encyclopedia.

At first, the children will probably need help to find the topic and to gather the facts that they need. With practice, they will be able to do this with some degree of independence. Make the children feel comfortable to ask for your help. The facts that they seek should be simple and should not require them to take notes. They can usually remember the information needed if they report back to the class directly.

Classification

Seven-year-old children are not yet ready to learn the detailed classification system of the library media center. They can understand the concept that each item has a specific location and know generally where to find materials that interest them. They can learn that each book has a spine label that designates its place on the shelf.

Second graders are highly competitive and enjoy group activities. They are also sensitive to the feelings and attitudes of others. The concept of the right and wrong way of doing things and the ability to play by set rules are beginning to emerge. These characteristics make the use of games for learning especially appropriate for children at this age. Team games generate lively participation. The game activity on page 59 builds an understanding of the organization of materials in the library media center.

Parts of a Book

A game activity such as the one on page 59 is also suggested for reviewing the parts of a book. After the children have been introduced to the various parts of a book, the game helps them to understand and review the function of the parts. They should know that a book has various parts that help the reader to understand and use its contents more fully.

Summary

In the second grade, as reading abilities increase, experience with a wide variety of materials awakens interest and motivates children to read independently. There is a close relationship between the program of the library media center and reading instruction.

The children are alert and active and want to become involved in what interests them. After listening to stories, they should be involved in discussion, dramatization, and drawing to help them to recall, summarize, and paraphrase what they have seen and heard.

SECOND GRADE LIBRARY SKILLS CHECKLIST AND ACTIVITIES

The following presents a sequential checklist of library and information skills to be developed at the second grade level and suggested activities for teaching specific skills. Each activity is keyed to a major skill objective at the second level and is ready for your immediate use or adaptation.

Library Skills Checklist
SECOND GRADE

Class _____

I. Location Skills
A. Card Catalog
   1. **Alphabetizing**
     a. Can locate a book in the easy section by the author's last name
     b. Knows that the spine label tells where the book is placed on the shelf
   2. **Subject Headings**
     a. Knows that books on specific subjects may be located in the nonfiction section of the library media center
     b. Can locate a book on a specific subject with the assistance of the library media specialist

B. Fiction and Nonfiction
   1. Can determine the difference between fiction and nonfiction in the most obvious instances
   2. Locates books in the easy collection
   3. Locates books with assistance in the fiction collection that he/she is able to read
   4. Locates materials on a topic with assistance in the nonfiction collection

C. Reference Collection
   1. **Encyclopedias**
     a. Can locate the primary level encyclopedias in the library media center
     b. Can locate the general encyclopedias in the reference collection
     c. Can find a topic in an encyclopedia with assistance
   2. **Dictionaries**
     a. Can locate the primary picture dictionaries in the library media center
     b. Can use alphabetical order and guide words in dictionary work

D. Periodicals
   1. Knows that the library media center has materials other than books
   2. Is familiar with the primary periodicals

E. Audiovisual Materials and Equipment
   1. Knows that the library media center has materials other than books
   2. Understands audiovisual presentations

Class _____

II. Interpretation Skills
A. Evaluation and Selection Techniques
1. Chooses books that he/she is able to read
2. Chooses books on subjects of interest and personal preference
3. Understands that there are various forms of literature

B. Parts of a Book
1. Can identify the cover
2. Can identify the spine and spine label
3. Can identify the title page
4. Can identify the title, author, and illustrator
5. Can identify the publisher, place of publication, and date of publication

C. Listening and Viewing Skills
1. Can attend to the sights and sounds of the instructional situation
2. Participates in a group discussion or other group activity
3. Can understand what is seen and heard
4. Can recall, summarize, and paraphrase what is listened to and viewed

D. Literature Appreciation
1. Knows that a variety of books are available
2. Can draw the point of the story into own experience

I. LOCATION SKILLS   A. Card Catalog

LOCATION GAME

The following team game develops the children's ability to locate books by the author's last name in the easy storybook section. It also promotes the understanding that the spine labels tell where the books are placed on the shelf.

Time: 30-minute sessions

Materials: $3'' \times 5''$ blank cards (20-30)

Felt-tip pen

Preparation: Make a set of 20 to 30 cards with one author's last name printed on each. The authors should be chosen from the easy storybook collection.

Activity Directions:

Describe how books are arranged in the easy storybook section. Say, "Books in the library media center are on the shelves in a certain order. What is the order?" Next, explain the order in which books are arranged: "Each book has a spine. Show me your spine. This is the spine of the book." Point to the spine of the book. "On the spine of the book is a label that is called the spine label. The first letter on the spine label stands for the section of the library. E is for the easy section." You may want to name other sections: R—reference and F—fiction. Ask, "What are the letters under the E? The beginning letters of the author's last name. Each shelf has a label with letters to help you find books quickly. The books are arranged on the shelves by the author's last name."

NOTE: *You may choose to give the introduction during a session prior to the session when the game is first played or in the same session as the game.*

Divide the class into two teams. Near the easy storybook section, have the teams face each other. Have a child from each team pick a card from the set of author cards and find a book by that author. The child then returns to his or her team with the book and reads the title and author. A marker may be inserted when the book is removed to make replacement easier. The first child to return to his or her team with the correct book wins a point for the team. The child then shelves the book in its proper place. This is repeated until all of the children have had a turn. The team with the most points wins.

Variations: This game may be repeated intermittently throughout the year. At first the game may be played with the children working with partners to find a book by a designated author. When they become more proficient at locating the books, they may play individually.

After the game has been played several times, the use of markers may be deleted from the game, requiring the children to return the books to the proper shelves without aid.

I. LOCATION SKILLS   A. Card Catalog

"MY COLLECTION"

This activity helps children to understand that books on a specific subject may be located in the nonfiction collection and enables them to locate nonfiction books of interest with the assistance of the library media specialist.

Time: 30 minutes

Materials: 5″ × 8″ cards

Felt-tip pen

Preparation: Note the call numbers of books on items usually collected by second grade children to enable you to pull them from the shelves quickly, for example, 737 coins, 745 dolls, 629 models, 552 rocks, 594 shells, 796 sports cards, 737 stamps.

Activity Directions:

Gather the children in a group near the nonfiction section of the library media center. Encourage them to talk about a collection that they have. As they name various collections, print the subjects on 5″ × 8″ cards. Choose subjects in which two or more students indicate an interest. When six to eight subjects of collections have been mentioned, explain that there are books in the library media center on many different subjects and that they will find books about their collections.

Place each subject card on a separate table and have the children sit at the table with the subject of a collection that they have or in which they are interested. With the children observing you, choose books on each subject from the nonfiction shelves and put them on the tables with the corresponding subject cards. Encourage the children to read, scan, and borrow the books.

Follow-up: Have the children bring in their collections or selected portions of their collections to display in the library media center. Label each collection with the contributor's name. You may want to entitle the display "Collections from (Mr. or) Mrs. _____'s Class." Books on the subjects of the collections may be displayed also.

I. LOCATION SKILLS   C. Reference Collection

LOCATING ENCYCLOPEDIAS

This activity enables the children to locate the encyclopedias in the library media center and to become familiar with the variety of subjects included in encyclopedias.

Time: 30 minutes

Materials: Several sets of encyclopedias on the primary level, such as *Childcraft, Brittanica Junior,* and *The Goldenbook Encyclopedia* (General encyclopedias may be used if primary encyclopedias are not available.)

Activity Directions:
Ask the children if they have used an encyclopedia. Encourage some to talk about the subjects that they have looked up and the information that they found. After a variety of subjects have been mentioned, ask the children how an encyclopedia is different from a nonfiction book. Develop the idea that an encyclopedia has information on many different subjects, whereas a book is usually about one subject. Also mention that a book is meant to be read all of the way through, but an encyclopedia is intended to be referred to for information on a certain subject.

Have the children gather around the encyclopedias in the reference collection. Give each child an encyclopedia. Have the children sit at tables and look through the encyclopedias to find as many different subjects as they can. Provide five minutes for this browsing. During this time draw attention to the continuation of paging from one volume to the next. Next, have the children name some of the subjects that they found in the encyclopedias.

Follow-up: Invite the children to come to the library media center to use encyclopedias when a question arises in class on a subject on which they need more information. Alert the classroom teacher to this service.

I. LOCATION SKILLS   D. Periodicals

EXPLORING PRIMARY MAGAZINES

This activity provides an opportunity for the children to become familiar with the primary magazines in the periodical collection.

Time: 30-minute sessions

Materials: Magazines from the periodical collection on the primary level, such as *Dynamite, Ranger Rick, Highlights*

Preparation: Display the primary level magazines to enable the children to browse through the collection. They might be put on tables around the room or along the windowsill.

Activity Directions:
Session I—Show the children where the magazines are kept and how they are arranged in the library media center: "The most current magazines are kept on the rack for you to find quickly and easily. All other magazines are kept in files on the shelves and are arranged alphabetically by title."

NOTE: *Periodical arrangement varies somewhat in particular situations. Describe these arrangements in the library media center.*

Select two different types of magazines to demonstrate the various kinds of articles in periodicals. For example, *Ranger Rick* has nature study information, whereas *Highlights* has stories and things to do. Read a short factual article from one magazine and a story from another.

Session II—To further demonstrate the range of information and format within periodicals, have the children browse through the primary periodicals.

Encourage the children to choose a magazine to take to a table to read. When they have finished, they may return to choose another.

After 15 minutes, have the children share what they have learned from the magazines with the class. Give the children an opportunity to show the magazine that they have been reading, to read the title, and to name something that they found in it. Encourage the children to keep comments brief in order to give every child a turn to share.

NOTE: *This activity may be repeated several times during the year.*

I. LOCATION SKILLS   E. Audiovisual Materials and Equipment

A STORY FILMSTRIP

This discussion activity helps children to discover that the library media center has materials other than books. It also helps them to understand more fully audiovisual presentations by providing opportunities to relate what they listen to and view to their own experiences.

Time: 30 minutes

Materials: Sound filmstrip—*Folktales of Different Lands.*
New York Times Educational Service, 1969.

This activity uses the filmstrip based on the book, *One Good Deed Deserves Another* by Katherine Evans. Chicago: Albert Whitman and Co., 1964.

Activity Directions:
Gather the children for a story. Show the book and explain that they are going to see a filmstrip of the story. Read the title of the book and ask if they know what it might mean. Choose several children to share their ideas. Have the children see if their ideas about the title change after viewing the story.

Show the filmstrip. Ask the children if they have changed their opinion of what the title means. Encourage them to discuss the good deeds in the story. Ask them if the thief got what he deserved and if the peasants got what they deserved. Have the children describe how they would feel if this happened to them. Encourage them to share any experiences they have had with good deeds being rewarded. Explain that they may look at the book and take turns borrowing it to read on their own.

Follow-up: The other filmstrips in this series may be used in a similar way. Give the children something to look for during the viewing that will be discussed afterwards. Have the book available for them to look at and to borrow.

The other filmstrips in this series are based on the following books:

Who Was Tricked? by James Cloyd Bowman.
Chicago: Albert Whitman and Co., 1966.

The Boy Who Cried Wolf by Katherine Evans.
Chicago: Albert Whitman and Co., 1960.

Stone Soup by Marcia Brown.
New York: Scribner's, 1947.

Variations: There are many excellent audiovisual materials available for second grade children on filmstrips as well as films and videotapes. When you use these materials, plan follow-up activities that give children opportunities to talk about what they have seen and heard.

II. INTERPRETATION SKILLS   A. Evaluation and Selection Techniques

SHARING BOOKS

This show-and-tell activity enhances the ability of the children to choose interesting books that they are able to read by coming in contact with a variety of books that their classmates are reading and enjoying.

Time: 30-minute sessions

Materials: Books that the children have read

Preparation: The children should have had several months of experience in selecting books under the individual guidance of the library media specialist.

Activity Directions:
Arrange the children in a circle on the floor or in low chairs. Explain that they may share a book that they have been reading with the class. Ask, "Who has a book that they would like to share?"

Choose one volunteer to stand, show the book, and name the title, author, and some part of the book that they especially remember. Encourage the children to tell where they found the books in the library media center. When they are finished they choose another child to take a turn sharing his or her book with the class.

> **NOTE:** *This activity may be repeated periodically throughout the year. There may not be time for all of the children to have a turn in each session. Each of the children should be given an opportunity to participate at some time.*
>
> *The sharing sessions should be spontaneous and enjoyable. Avoid the tone of a formal book report.*

II. INTERPRETATION SKILLS   B. Parts of a Book

"WHAT PART?"

This team game provides practice in identifying the following parts of a book: cover, spine, spine label, title page, title, author, illustrator, publisher, place of publication, and date of publication. Games stimulate interest in review tasks.

NOTE: *A similar game is played in first grade using six parts of a book. In the second grade, the same game is extended to include 10 parts of a book and the competition of team play.*

Time: 30-minute sessions
Materials: Slips of paper with the name of a different part of a book on each
Preparation: For several weeks, at the beginning of a story reading, introduce the parts of a book. Introduce one or two each week until all have been identified. Make up the slips of paper with the name of a different part of a book on each.
Activity Directions:
Have the parts of a book listed on separate slips of paper. Divide the class into two teams by counting off 1-2. Have team 1 sit on one side and team 2 opposite them with their backs to each other.

Choose a player from each team to start the game. Have the children draw one slip of paper with a part of a book and describe the part to their teammates. The first team to guess the part correctly wins a point. In case of a tie, both teams get a point. If the members of either team become too noisy or unruly, a point is deducted from their score.

The child with the correct answer takes the next turn to represent a part of a book for his or her team to guess. Continue until all of the parts are given at least twice and all of the children have had a turn. At the end of the game, the team with the most points wins.

Follow-up: This game may be repeated several times throughout the year.

Variation: Role playing, as in the game of charades, may be used to demonstrate the parts of a book instead of depicting it in a word description.

II. INTERPRETATION SKILLS   C. Listening and Viewing Skills

DRAMATIZING A STORY

This activity builds children's ability to attend to the sights and sounds of the instructional situation as they recall, summarize, and paraphrase what they see and hear.

Time: Four 30-minute sessions
Materials: *The Fool of the World and The Flying Ship*
                 by Arthur Ransome.
                 New York: Farrar, Straus and Giroux, 1968.
Activity Directions:
Sessions I and II—During the first two sessions, read the story to the class. Explain that they are going to dramatize the story, and ask them to picture how the action will be played while the story is being read.

Sessions III and IV—At the beginning of the third session, have the children choose parts. Review the story by showing the pictures and have the children name the characters on each page. Write the characters on a blackboard as they are named. After all of the characters have been listed, have the children volunteer for the parts. Write the name of the child who will play the part next to the name of the character on the blackboard.

Then arrange the class in a large circle with the playing area in the center. Have the children playing parts together sit near each other. The children not participating in a skit are the audience, except when they are playing their parts.

Present the rule that only the child assigned to the part speaks and acts. If that player needs assistance to recall the part, he or she asks for help and chooses a classmate to coach.

The complete dramatization of this story usually takes two sessions.

Follow-up: Many books lend themselves to dramatization. This activity may be repeated with various stories throughout the year. Choose books with many characters to ensure that every child has a part to play. The following books are recommended for dramatization:

A Story, A Story by Gail E. Haley.
New York: Atheneum, 1970.

Nine in a Line by Ann Kirn.
New York: W. W. Norton, 1966.

Too Much Noise by Ann McGovern.
Boston: Houghton Mifflin, 1967.

II. INTERPRETATION SKILLS   C. Listening and Viewing Skills

ROLE PLAYING

This dramatization activity helps children to concentrate on what they hear and see so that they may more fully understand and interpret it. Through role playing, they are given opportunities to recall, summarize, and paraphrase what they have listened to and viewed.

Time: 30 minutes
Materials: *I Am Your Misfortune*
                    retold by Marguerita Rudolph.
                    New York: Seabury Press, 1968.

Activity Directions:
Gather the children around for a story. Explain that it is about two brothers whose feelings change as their situations change. Ask the children to be aware of the feelings of the brothers throughout the story. Read the story with expression, showing the pictures as you proceed.

After the story has been read, show the illustration at the beginning of the book. Ask the children how they think each brother felt. Choose a child to describe through role playing how the rich brother felt. Next, choose another child to role play the poor brother's feelings. Continue until all of the children have had an opportunity to role play the feelings displayed by the brothers throughout the story.

Variation: After each child has role played the feeling, you may want the entire class to display the feeling by their facial expressions. This involves the participation of all of the children throughout the activity.

Follow-up: Role playing may be used to express feelings and actions in stories that you read during the year. It is not always necessary to build an entire lesson on role playing. For example, you may want to have the children role play a particularly vivid or puzzling part of a story to increase their understanding.

II. INTERPRETATION SKILLS   C. Listening and Viewing Skills

DRAW THE ENDING!

This drawing activity helps children to concentrate on what they hear and see so that they may more fully understand and interpret. Drawing gives them opportunities to recall, summarize, and paraphrase what they have listened to and viewed.

Time: Two 30-minute sessions

Materials: *The Enormous Crocodile* by Roald Dahl.
                 New York: Alfred A. Knopf, 1978.
                 Drawing paper
                 Crayons

Activity Directions:

Gather the children around for a story. Explain that the story is about a very mean, nasty crocodile and that the author has decided what he thinks should happen to the crocodile at the end of the story. Tell the children to listen carefully so that they can decide what they think should happen at the end of the story.

Read the story with expression, showing the amusing illustrations as you proceed. This is an outrageously humorous and somewhat shocking story that is highly appealing to most second graders. The story will probably take more than one session to complete. Read approximately two-thirds of the book during the first session and finish the story at the beginning of the second session.

After you have read the story, ask the children if they would have ended the story the way the author did. Have them sit at tables and draw a picture of how they would have ended the story. Allow 10 to 15 minutes for drawing the pictures. Give each child an opportunity to show his or her drawing and describe the ending for the story that they illustrated.

Variations: Many books lend themselves to this type of activity. *Bumps in the Night* by Harry Allard (New York: Doubleday & Co., 1979) is another book that can be used for drawing endings. In this case, read to page 23 and have the children draw what they think is the ending of the story. After they have described how they would end the story, complete the reading of the book.

II. INTERPRETATION SKILLS   D. Literature Appreciation

FOLK TALES

This activity familiarizes children with a variety of books. It also offers opportunities for the children to incorporate the point of the story into their own experience in order to find meaning.*

Time: 20- to 30-minute sessions

Materials: *Why Mosquitoes Buzz in People's Ears* by Verna Aardema.
        New York: Dial Press, 1978. (West African)
        World map
        2 sheets 9″ × 12″ construction paper
        Felt-tip pen
        Ball of colored yarn
        Box of tacks with plastic heads

Preparation: Make a bulletin board displaying a simple world map on the upper portion and two sheets of light-colored construction paper on the lower portion. Have a ball of colored yarn and a box of tacks available. Above the map, write the title for the bulletin board, "STORIES FROM OTHER COUNTRIES." See follow-up activities.

Activity Directions:

Gather the children around for a story. They usually sit on the floor or on low chairs around the library media specialist's chair. Explain that in some countries there are no scientists that observe, experiment, and explain why things happen. In those places, storytellers often make up tales to explain things. This is a story to explain *Why Mosquitoes Buzz in People's Ears*. Read the story, noting the use of sound effects in the text. Show the illustrations after reading each page, drawing attention to unique features in the pictures. In this case, draw attention to the techniques used to indicate action.

After the story, have the children discuss how misunderstandings occur and how the truth is discovered. After discussing the incidents in the story, have the children talk about a misunderstanding in their own experience and explain how they discovered the truth.

Follow-up: Storybooks of folk tales from other countries may be read on a continuing basis. Each story may be introduced with brief background comments about the country's storytelling culture. These facts can often be found on the cover leaf or in the introductory statements of the book. Unique

---

*This lesson was developed by Frankie Wideman, Library Media Specialist, Smith School, East Brunswick, New Jersey.

features in the illustrations should be noted during the reading of the text. After the story, a discussion question should be presented which draws the point of the story into the children's experiences.

The following books are recommended for this activity:

Duffy and the Devil by Harve and Margot Zemach.
New York: Farrar, Straus, and Giroux, 1973. (Cornish)

The Hole in the Dike by Norma Green.
New York: Thomas Y. Crowell, 1975. (Dutch)

I Am Your Misfortune retold by Marguerita Rudolph.
New York: Seabury Press, 1968. (Lithuanian)

Stone Soup by Marcia Brown.
New York: Scribner's, 1947. (Swedish)

Three Gold Pieces by Aliki.
New York: Pantheon Books, 1967. (Greek)

Bulletin Board: After each story is read, use a felt-tip pen to list the title and country of origin on the construction paper under the map. A piece of yarn may then be strung from the title of the story to the location of the country on the world map using a tack at each end.

IV. THIRD GRADE

Exploring the Entire Library Media Center Collection

Third grade is a period of transition in the use of the library media center. The children gradually change from using the materials in the easy collection almost exclusively to using the entire library media center collection. During this transition period, they freely move back and forth between the different sections, using materials of varying levels of difficulty and interest. The children have a sense of achievement, knowing that they may choose materials from the nonfiction and fiction collections.

This chapter provides:

- A description of third graders' needs in terms of the library program
- A checklist of library skills to be developed at the third level
- Activities for teaching specific skills

THE THIRD GRADE PROGRAM

In order for the children to find materials outside of the easy collection, they need to have a general idea of how the materials are categorized and where the categories are located on the shelves of the library media center. Avoid going into a detailed description of library classification at this time. The children are not capable of understanding, nor are they interested in, an indepth study of the Dewey Decimal System. What they need is a general idea of what things are available for them and where these things are.

The eight-year-old children are entering a stage of development during which they will develop the ability to handle classification. During the early phase of this stage, they can understand the general concept of classification and use of categories.

Fiction and Nonfiction

The two main categories of the library media center materials are fiction and nonfiction. This is very important for the children to understand. It is the basis of the Dewey Decimal System. The activity "Indians of North America," on page 76, helps children develop the ability to distinguish between fiction and nonfiction. Give them additional opportunities to determine the category of the book that they are reading. Continue to bring this to their attention both formally and informally throughout the year.

The difference between fiction and nonfiction is often confusing to children. Fictional stories sometimes seem quite real, while folk tales and fairy tales are considered nonfiction. This may be clarified by explaining that folk tales and fairy tales are traditional literature passed down from one generation to another and considered part of the cultural heritage of the people. By comparing a folk tale with a fictional story created by one author, the children can more fully understand how the two types of literature fit into the categories of fiction and nonfiction.

Several activities in this chapter provide opportunities to analyze fiction to determine what part of the story is based on true facts and what part is the creation of the author's imagination. In this way, the children can learn to interpret what they read and avoid misunderstandings that develop through over-generalizing the categories of fiction and nonfiction. Avoid misleading, oversimplified definitions, such as the distinction that nonfiction is true and fiction is false. This might result in misconceptions and a general confusion of the distinction between the categories.

Call Numbers

The children may be introduced to the fact that the call numbers of fiction and nonfiction differ. They can understand that the purpose of nonfiction call numbers is to pull together books on the same topic and that books are arranged on the shelves according to the call number. "Call Numbers Game," on page 77, helps children learn the order of books on the shelves.

Card Catalog

In the third grade, children learn the procedure to locate a book. They learn to go to the card catalog, look up a topic, jot down the call number, and go to the shelf to find a book on the topic. The activities "Which Drawer?" and "Call Numbers Game," on pages 75 and 77, give third graders opportunities to practice this procedure. At first, this is complicated for all of the children.

They need a great amount of assistance and encouragement. Don't expect them to independently use the card catalog immediately.

Develop the children's confidence in their own ability to find materials. They become discouraged when they can't find materials quickly. This feeling of discouragement often returns when they attempt to use the card catalog at another time. If they experience success in finding materials, their self-confidence increases and they develop a positive attitude toward their ability to use the library media center. Help a child who is experiencing difficulty by walking him or her through the process.

The most effective time to instruct a child on how to use the card catalog to locate a book is when he or she is interested in a topic and highly motivated to find information. This encourages the child to continue to push on through the steps of locating information when a problem is encountered.

The children will not all learn this skill at the same rate. Some children will be able to locate books long before others have understood the procedure. Have those who have mastered the technique help their classmates to locate materials. Be certain that at some point during the year you individually assist each child to follow the procedure of locating a nonfiction book through the card catalog. If a child is always helped by another child, he or she may miss one step that is crucial to the process. By the end of the year, all of the children should have had the experience of finding a call number of a subject in the card catalog and locating the corresponding nonfiction material.

Biography

The children will need to understand that the nonfiction collection includes a biography section. This section of the library media center is a source of unique, interesting information that is often overlooked in the third grade.

Draw attention to the biography section by introducing books about people who have led unusual or remarkable lives and books that the children can read independently. Eight-year-olds have a new awareness of individual differences. They can understand that people have a variety of opportunities and make different choices about how they will lead their lives. At this age, the children are interested in famous people. Introduce biographies in which the famous person's area of expertise is within the realm of the children's experience and understanding, such as famous American Indians, founding fathers of the United States, or popular sports figures.

Reference

The reference collection will become an increasingly more important source of information for third graders. Do not expect third grade children to do in-depth reports using multiple sources. Combining information from several sources is a complex skill that is developed in stages over a period of several years. They can use one source to find information on a topic of personal interest or in answer to a question. This is the initial step toward building research and reporting capabilities.

The eight-year-old child's attention span has increased as has the ability to attend to detail. Third graders are interested in new things and eager to expand their knowledge. When a topic is discussed in the classroom, the children often want to come to the library media center to gather additional information. Once their interest is sparked, they naturally want to know more.

Third graders can understand that reference books are meant to be referred to and not read all of the way through. They begin to use reference books when they want quick, comprehensive information on a topic. Encyclopedias are an excellent source for the children to use to expand their understanding of a topic. Alert the children to the fact that encyclopedias have information on people, places, and things. Things, in this case, include events.

Third graders should be given opportunities to survey general topics and to select what they consider important or find interesting. Research can be an expansive experience for them. Avoid structure that restricts their inquisitive nature. They need opportunities to develop broad understandings, not to be constrained by narrow, adult-directed questions. Allow third graders to follow their own interests, from which they can develop meaningful questions of their own. For example, at this age a child who expresses an interest in horses may want to know anything and everything about horses. Children in the third grade are interested in expanding their general information base.

Provide opportunities for the children to share what they have learned with their classmates. Create an atmosphere of acceptance when children are reporting on information that they have found. You will want to question an occasional misinterpreted fact, but generally accept whatever information the child has considered significant and has selected to share with his or her classmates.

When children are asked to gather information and to report on a topic, their initial tendency is to copy word for word from the encyclopedia or any other book that they are using. They naturally feel that they cannot possibly word the information as well as the text. It is important at this early stage for them to develop confidence in their own ability to select what is important to report about a topic and to say it in their own words. An accepting environment for sharing the information gathered enhances their self-confidence. The "Research and Report" activity, on page 85, requires that the children, after reading an encyclopedia article, close the encyclopedia and write the information they recall. In this way the children practice reporting from memory. They apply the skills of recall, summarizing, and paraphrasing to accomplish the task.

Making Their Own Books

By third grade, the children have been introduced to all of the parts of a book. The activity "Create Your Own Book," on page 82, gives the task of making their own books, incorporating all the various parts that they have previously learned. In this way they individually work through each function as they see how it applies to their book. This prepares them for using the various parts of a book in the fourth, fifth, and sixth grades. If they fully understand the function of each part and know the structure of books, they can use the parts when they need to. For example, in the fourth grade the children will use indexes to find information in nonfiction books. If third grade children have made simple indexes for their own books, they understand the function of indexes and will more easily learn to use them.

Beyond the structural and functional learning that takes place in making their own books, the children derive great pleasure in the task. Allow them to choose the kind of book they will write. Some children may want to write nonfiction books, such as "How to Make a Pizza" or "My Dog Tuffy." Others may write a fantasy, and still others a humorous nonsense story. By giving a general direction, you can leave the choice of the kind of book to write to the individual child. For example, ask them to write a book for a younger child.

Sometimes children have trouble getting started with a story. You might want to use story starters to suggest ideas. Story starters can be pictures that show action, as in children's periodicals. Also, phrases to begin a story may be suggested. For example, say, "It was a dark, still night when ...," or, "It all began that sunny morning ..."

Story starters sometimes inhibit creativity rather than stimulating it in third graders. The children sometimes interpret the suggested story starter as a direction on how to start their book and reject their own ideas in favor of the story starter. You might prefer to individually assist children who are experiencing difficulty in getting started.

The children rarely plunge into writing. Allow for a period of pre-writing. Time is needed to collect thoughts and to plan how to proceed before writing can begin. Most will start writing after 5 to 10 minutes. Even after they start to write, they will occasionally stop to think and to read over what they have written.

The children will vary in the rate at which they write and in the length of the books they produce. Make provision for these differences. Some will need more time than others to complete their stories. Although the activity directions call for a specific amount of time and for a certain amount of paper, be flexible in order to accommodate the needs of all of the children.

There is some confusion and controversy about whether to correct children's writing. The children generally want their writing to be spelled correctly and worded so that others can understand their meaning. On the other hand, they are sometimes offended and disappointed by being handed back a paper covered with red marks. You might try reading the paper over with the child, correcting errors together as you read. This requires that you meet with each child individually, which is most effective but not always possible.

You might explain to the children that all writers have an editor who proofreads books before printing them. You can be the editor of their books. Give the children an opportunity to make a fresh final copy of their writing. Don't insist that the children always recopy their work, however. This can become tedious and tiresome for children at this age, and it quickly dampens the enthusiasm of young writers.

After the books are finished, provide an opportunity for the children to have a read-around, a session where they can read each other's books. The children are proud of their work and derive great pleasure in sharing it with others. They are usually especially appreciative of another child's work since they have shared the experience and can understand the effort involved. Provide an accepting, appreciative climate for a successful read-around.

The children will take future writing tasks more seriously if they see results in their work. By binding the books and adding them to the library media center as a special collection, the children can experience the sense of accomplishment of an author. This opportunity to identify with an author gives children an appreciation for the effort and creativity that goes into book writing and publishing.

Reading

At eight years of age, children are in a period of slow, steady growth that is most conducive to learning and improving the basic communication skills of reading, writing, listening, and speaking. Physically, most children at this age are ready for more extended periods of concentration and are able to perform more precise tasks.

Reading to the children continues to be an important part of the library media center program. As they become more competent, independent readers, they need to become acquainted with the characteristics of the books in the fiction collection. These books have more fully depicted characters, thoroughly described settings, and extensively developed plots. Fiction books have a series of chapters, and the illustrations are fewer and more subdued.

Third graders sometimes are not motivated to stay with a fiction book to the end. They will read a few chapters and lose interest. You may want to read an entire book aloud to give them an understanding of the full sweep of a sustained fiction book. In this way, the children are encouraged to read a book all of the way through. Once they become more familiar with the format, many do not want a book to end and will reread it or ask for a sequel.

Follow-up Activities

Reacting to what is read and viewed through follow-up activities is extremely important in third grade. Children's reading and writing skills, as well as their use of language, have improved sufficiently to be applied to learning. Eight-year-olds are noisy and argumentative, but also alert, friendly, and interested in people. Peers become important and the children are aware of different points of view.

When planning follow-up activities, you should consider these characteristics. In a discussion, the children will usually keep to the main point, listen to each other's comments, and build on them. Opportunities to talk about what they have read and seen on television or in films helps children to understand and to interpret meaning. Discussion, both formal and casual, prepares the way for analysis and evaluation. In this way, the children begin to develop both abilities to discriminate and techniques for making choices in selecting media.

Extending

In the second grade, the children participated in activities to develop the ability to recall, summarize, and paraphrase. In the third grade, opportunities to develop the ability to *extend*, or to use their own ideas, are added to these three. *Recall* is thinking back on what was seen and heard to remember the events, facts, and feelings. *Summarizing* is thinking of what is recalled in a manageable, capsulized form. *Paraphrasing* is talking about what is recalled and summarizing in one's own way.

Extending is taking the verbal description beyond what is recalled on to creating some new idea or thought. It is extending the ideas of another by adding one's own thoughts. The "Story Extension," on page 86, gives children opportunities to extend what they have read. After listening to a story, which is somewhat open-ended, the children are asked to create their own ending. For example, the story *The Abominable Swamp Man* by Gail Haley ends with only one of three wishes being used. The children are asked to continue the story in their own way using the other wishes.

You may have the children extend stories and information in less formal ways throughout the year. Once you are aware of extending, you will find many opportunities for developing this ability. Extending is a delightfully creative activity. The freedom of this activity encourages individuality. An almost unlimited variety of possible ideas can be used in extending. The children might create extensions in a variety of modes using science fiction, fantasy, or a realistic extension. Third graders derive great pleasure in sharing their extensions with each other.

Writing and Drawing

In the third grade, writing and drawing are very closely connected. The children are increasingly more able to use writing to communicate thoughts, but they usually want to include a drawing to complete the communication. Many of the activities in this section incorporate the use of writing and drawing. For example, the children illustrate the books that they write. When they use an encyclopedia to find information on a topic, they are asked to report through drawing as well as writing.

Throughout the third grade, have the children respond to books and audiovisual presentations by using a combination of writing and drawing. Provide opportunities for the children to share their communications with classmates.

Summary

Third grade is a transition year during which the children emerge from almost exclusive use of the easy collection and begin to use the entire library media center collection. They learn the simple, general organization of materials, but not a detailed study of the classification system. The children have opportunities to react to what they see and hear through a combination of writing and drawing that they share with their classmates. They are encouraged to extend what they see and hear with their own individual ideas.

THIRD GRADE LIBRARY SKILLS
CHECKLIST AND ACTIVITIES

The following presents a sequential checklist of library and information skills to be developed at the third grade level and suggested activities for teaching specific skills. Each activity is keyed to a major skill objective at the third level and is ready for your immediate use or adaptation.

Library Skills Checklist
THIRD GRADE

Class_____

I. Location Skills
A. Card Catalog
1. Understands that every book and most other material in the library media center collection has at least one card in the card catalog
2. Can locate materials using call numbers on catalog cards

   a. **Alphabetizing**
- (1) Knows library books are shelved alphabetically using the author's last name
- (2) Knows biography is shelved alphabetically by the subject's last name

   b. **Subject Headings**
- (1) Knows the card catalog has subject cards
- (2) Can look up a subject and find a call number
- (3) Can locate a book on a subject using the card catalog with some assistance

   c. **Descriptive Information**
- (1) Knows there is information on the catalog card that tells about the book
- (2) Knows the parts of a book that are listed on the catalog card

B. Fiction and Nonfiction
1. Can define the difference between fiction and nonfiction
2. Knows that the two main categories in the library media center are fiction and nonfiction

C. Dewey Decimal System
1. Is familiar with call numbers and their relation to the location of the book on the shelf
2. Understands the general shelf arrangement of library media center materials

D. Reference Collection
1. Knows the difference between the reference collection and the regular collection
2. Can locate the reference collection
3. Knows reference sources are meant to be referred to, not read all the way through
4. Can locate information in encyclopedias and dictionaries with some assistance

   a. **Encyclopedias**
- (1) Can use the alphabetical arrangement of the general encyclopedia to locate a subject
- (2) Can use a general encyclopedia to find information on a topic
- (3) Knows there are special-subject encyclopedias in the reference collection
- (4) Knows encyclopedias are a source of information about people, places, and things

   b. **Dictionaries**
- (1) Can locate the unabridged dictionary in the library media center
- (2) Can use the abridged and unabridged dictionaries to find word definitions

Class_____

E. Biographical Sources
1. Can locate information about a person with some assistance
2. Knows biography is shelved alphabetically by the subject's last name

F. Periodicals
1. Is familiar with the primary periodicals and, in addition, some intermediate periodicals
2. Knows there are special-subject periodicals

G. Indexes
1. Knows that an important part of a book is the index
2. Knows that some nonfiction books have indexes
3. Knows that indexes are in the backs of books

H. Audiovisual Materials and Equipment
1. Knows the library media center has materials other than books
2. Understands audiovisual presentations

II. Interpretation Skills
A. Evaluation and Selection Techniques
1. Is familiar with various forms of literature
2. Knows some favorite authors and their works
3. With some help, can select materials that he/she can read
4. Shows discrimination in selecting books

B. Parts of a Book
1. Can identify the table of contents
2. Can identify the dedication
3. Can identify the preface
4. Can identify the appendix
5. Can identify the glossary
6. Can identify the bibliography
7. Can identify the index

C. Research and Reporting Techniques
1. Can look up information on a topic in a general encyclopedia
2. Can find nonfiction books on a specific topic
3. Is acquainted with bibliographies in books

D. Listening and Viewing Skills
1. Participates in a group discussion by following the rules that (a) only one person speaks at a time, (b) everyone listen to the speaker, and (c) responses to discussion questions should be relevant
2. Can attend to the sights and sounds of the instructional situation
3. Can understand and interpret what is seen and heard
4. Can recall, summarize, paraphrase, and extend what is listened to and viewed

E. Literature Appreciation
1. Is familiar with characters, plot, and setting of fiction
2. Is familiar with many different types of literature

I. LOCATION SKILLS   A. Card Catalog

WHICH DRAWER?

This activity acquaints children with the alphabetical arrangement of cards in the card catalog.

Time: 30 minutes

Materials: One piece of oaktag, 24″ × 36″
Marking pens

Preparation: Make a chart of the drawer labels of the card catalog.

Activity Directions:

Explain that the card catalog has cards for all of the materials in the library media center. Ask the children if they know how the cards are arranged. Have several children describe the alphabetical arrangement of the cards. If the children have difficulty doing this, describe some of the ways the catalog might be arranged, but is not. For example, say, "It is not arranged by the number on the spine labels of the books. It is not arranged by the type of book, such as fiction, nonfiction, easy. It is arranged alphabetically by the first line on the card."

Show the chart of the drawer labels. Choose a child to read each label as you point to it. As the labels are being read, have a child name something that would be in the drawer.

Explain that they are going to play a guessing game. Describe something that would be in one of the drawers without naming what you are thinking of. For example, say, "I am thinking of something very large, gray, with a long trunk." Choose one child to tell what it is and to come forward to point out the drawer where the subject would be found. Give several examples and then have the child who answered correctly describe a subject. Continue until all of the children have had a turn to guess and describe a topic.

Variations: List 20 to 30 describable subjects on the chalkboard. The children may choose one of these subjects instead of thinking of their own. Check off each subject as it is described in the game.

I. LOCATION SKILLS   A. Card Catalog

USING SUBJECT HEADINGS

This group activity acquaints children with the subject cards in the card catalog. It provides practice in looking up a subject to find the call number. It also requires the children to use the alphabetical arrangement of the card catalog.

Time: 30 minutes

Materials: One piece of oaktag, 24″ × 36″
                   Marking pens
                   Chalkboard and chalk
                   10 slips of paper

Preparation: During prior sessions play the shelf-arrangement game, "Call Numbers" on page 77, with all combinations. Make a chart showing the drawer labels of the card catalog. (See the activity "Which Drawer?" for learning alphabetizing of the card catalog.)

Activity Directions:

Explain to the children that they may use the card catalog to lead them to materials on topics in which they are interested. Have the children think of some things that they would like to find out about. As they name the topics, choose six to eight that would be appropriate subject headings found in the card catalog. List these six to eight subjects on the chalkboard.

Present the chart showing a replica of the drawer labels of the card catalog. Briefly review the alphabetical arrangement of the drawer labels.

Divide the class into groups of three or four children. Write each subject heading on a slip of paper. Give each group a slip of paper with a subject heading. Have the children in each group decide which card catalog drawer would have the subject and send one child to get the proper drawer. Ask the children to locate the subject card and find the call number. One child from each group may write the call number on the chalkboard beside the corresponding subject. Offer assistance to groups experiencing difficulty.

When all of the groups have completed their task, review the entire list. Have each group read the subject heading with the call number and tell about how they located it.

I. LOCATION SKILLS   B. Fiction and Nonfiction

INDIANS OF NORTH AMERICA

This activity helps children to understand that the two main categories in the library media center collection are fiction and nonfiction. It also demonstrates the differences between fiction and nonfiction materials.

Time: Two 30-minute sessions

Materials: Books on Indians of North America from the fiction and
                  nonfiction collections of the library media center

Preparation: Prepare a display of books about Indians of North America. Include in the display fiction about Indians, Indian folk tales, nonfiction titles from the 970's, and biographies of famous Indians.

NOTE: *This activity is most effective when it is coordinated with a topic studied in social studies or science. For example, this lesson is especially meaningful when the children are learning about Indian life.*

Activity Directions:

Session I—Ask the children to explain the difference between fiction and nonfiction materials. Encourage several children to share their ideas. Develop the concept that in fictional stories the author has used his or her imagination to create a story with characters and a plot, whereas nonfiction books have facts and information on a certain topic. Explain that the differences between fiction and nonfiction are sometimes confusing because fictional stories often seem very real.

Point out that folk tales are considered nonfiction because they are traditional literature, passed from one generation to another, which are considered part of the cultural heritage of the people. Have the children discuss how folk tales are different from a fictional story created by one author. Next, have the children describe biographies and point out that biography is nonfiction.

List the following on a chart or a chalkboard:

BIOGRAPHY   —FICTION
FICTION   —NONFICTION
FICTION   —FOLK TALES

Have several children explain the differences between each type of material.

Encourage the children to choose and borrow a book from the display on Indians of North America, which they will talk about during the following session. Explain that the books are fiction and nonfiction.

Session II—Briefly review the differences between fiction and nonfiction. Give each child an opportunity to tell about the book that he or she borrowed. Have each decide whether the book is fiction or nonfiction and how the book might be used. For example, a child might say that a book is used to gather information for reporting or that it is used to read for fun. Then encourage each child to tell briefly about something that he or she found interesting in the book.

Follow-up: This activity may be repeated with other topics. Choose topics that the children are learning about in a subject area.

Variation: The children may tell about the books that they have returned at any given session. The random topics do not generally detract from the distinction between fiction and nonfiction.

I. LOCATION SKILLS   C. Dewey Decimal System

CALL NUMBERS GAME

The following group game familiarizes children with the call numbers and their relation to the location of a book on the shelf. Over a period of time, it will help students understand the general shelf arrangement of library media center materials.*

Time: 30-minute sessions

Materials: 5″ × 8″ cards (35-70)
                  Felt-tip pen

Preparation: Using the 5″ × 8″ cards, make up several sets of 5 to 10 cards that have call numbers that include author letters. Include in these sets:

- A set with a card for each section of the Dewey Decimal System
- A set that divides one of the sections into smaller subsections, such as: 501, 532, 551, 560, 594
- A set with the same Dewey numbers using different author letters, such as: 636   636   636   636   636
  AND, CAL, HOV, MIL,   SMI
- Sets with call numbers for each of the following sections of the library media center collection: fiction, biography, audiovisual materials, reference

Activity Directions:

Give one set of cards with call numbers to some of the children in the class. Ask these children to be books or other materials on a shelf, displaying their call numbers on their spine labels.

Have the children at their seats put the "books" in order by identifying which comes first. That "book" moves to the beginning of the line. Continue until all of the "books" are in order, and then have the "books" choose other children to take their places until all have had a turn.

NOTE: *This game may be repeated intermittently throughout the school year by using call numbers from the various sections of the library media center collection with increasing complexity.*

Variations: The call number cards may be mixed up and the children asked to find books with corresponding call numbers. A marker may be put in place of the book to be returned to its proper place, after showing the class the book and corresponding call number card.

I. LOCATION SKILLS   D. Reference Collection

COMPARING BOOKS

This activity helps children to understand the difference between the reference collection and the regular collection. It introduces the concept that reference sources are meant to be referred to and not read all the way through.

---

*This lesson was developed by Frankie Wideman, Library Media Specialist, Smith School, East Brunswick, New Jersey.

The activity also provides children with opportunities to practice locating and interpreting information in encyclopedias.

Time: 30 minutes

Materials: Encyclopedias from the library media center reference collection

Activity Directions:

Have the children discuss the difference between a book from the regular collection that you read all the way through and a reference book that you refer to for only the information that you need. Point out that this is the reason why reference books are called as such.

Pass an encyclopedia to each child. Allow a few minutes for them to leaf through it and to note interesting topics. Ask the children how the topics are arranged. Point out the alphabetical order that is used. Describe the use of guide words by explaining that the words at the top of each page help you to find a topic alphabetically.

Have the children look through the encyclopedias to find different ways of presenting information on a topic. List the items on the chalkboard as they are named by the children, such as pictures, maps, charts, words.

I. LOCATION SKILLS   E. Biographical Sources

PEOPLE IN BIOGRAPHY

This activity acquaints children with the biography collection of the library media center. It also helps children understand that biographies are arranged alphabetically by the last name of the subject. Practice in locating biographies is provided, and the children are encouraged to borrow and to read biographies.

Time: Two 30-minute sessions

Materials: The biography collection of the library media center
Benjamin Franklin by Ingri and Edgar Parin D'Aulaire.
New York: Doubleday and Company, 1950.
Pocahontas by same authors, 1949.
George Washington by same authors, 1936.

Activity Directions:

Session I—Explain that people live their lives in many different ways. Books that tell about the lives of people who have done unusual or remarkable things are especilly interesting. Ask the children if they know what these books are called. Write "Biography" on a chart on the chalkboard. Encourage the children to give examples of biographies that they have read and seen in television programs or films.

Ask the children to describe the difference between fictional characters and people in biography. Choose several children to share their ideas and to give examples.

Write a call number for a biography from the library media center on the chalkboard. Explain that the letters do not refer to the author's name, but to the subject's name. Give several examples, comparing them with call numbers from the fiction collection.

Show the biographies by the D'Aulaires. Tell about each briefly, showing some of the illustrations. Read the first five to eight pages of *Benjamin Franklin*.

Direct the children to select a biography from the library media center collection that they will read and tell about during the next session. Assist them individually to locate books that they can read.

Session II—Provide an opportunity for each child to tell about the life of the person in the biography that they borrowed and read.

I. LOCATION SKILLS   H. Audiovisual Materials and Equipment

INTERRELATED FORMATS

This activity acquaints the children with materials other than books in the library media center. It also demonstrates that materials of various formats are interrelated.

Time: Two 30-minute sessions

Materials: Sound filmstrip—*Misty of Chincoteaque*
by Marguerite Henry,
Miller Brody Productions, 1974.

Books—*Misty of Chincoteaque* by Marguerite Henry.
New York: Rand McNally, 1947.

Stormy, Misty's Foal by Marguerite Henry.
New York: Rand McNally, 1963.

Sea Star, Orphan of Chincoteaque
by Marguerite Henry.
New York: Rand McNally, 1949.

The Pictorial Life Story of Misty by Marguerite Henry.
New York: Rand McNally, 1976.

The Wild Ponies of Assateaque Island
by Donna K. Grosvenor. (Books for Young Explorers.)
National Geographic Society, 1975.

Activity Directions:

Session I—Before viewing the filmstrip, explain that Chincoteaque Island is an actual place off the coast of Virginia that has herds of wild ponies. This is a fictional story based on an actual place, real events, and people who live there. Ask the children to see whether they can tell what part of the story is based on real facts and what part is written from the author's imagination.

Show the first part of the filmstrip. After part one, encourage the children to discuss what they think are true facts in the story and what parts are the author's creation.

Session II—Have the books about Misty on display along with other nonfiction materials on horses, fictional horse stories, and other titles by Marguerite Henry.

Select the books listed under materials from the display and describe each one briefly, showing the illustrations. Ask the children to name some of the differences between reading the book *Misty* and watching the filmstrip. Next, have the children consider how the other books on the display are related to each other.

Show the conclusion of the filmstrip. Encourage the children to browse and to borrow the books on display.

Follow-up: This activity may be used with other audiovisual materials. Always provide an opportunity for the children to discuss the meaning of what is listened to and viewed.

II. INTERPRETATION SKILLS   A. Evaluation and Selection Techniques

MEET THE AUTHOR

This activity introduces some authors and their books and provides opportunities for the children to develop some favorites.

Time: 30 minutes

Materials: *Henry Huggins* by Beverly Cleary.
New York: William Morrow and Co., 1950.

The Mouse and the Motorcycle by Beverly Cleary.
New York: William Morrow and Co., 1965.

Ribsy by Beverly Cleary.
New York: William Morrow and Co., 1964.

Runaway Ralph by Beverly Cleary.
New York: William Morrow and Co., 1970.

Socks by Beverly Cleary.
New York: William Morrow and Co., 1973.

Other books by Beverly Cleary that the children can read

Activity Directions:

Gather the children around for a story. On a table beside you, display several books by Beverly Cleary. Explain that all of the books were written by the same author. Tell the children that they will probably be able to read the books with some help.

Hold up each book and tell about it by briefly describing an amusing or enticing event in the story. Show several illustrations and explain that they are meant for the reader of the book and not intended for a large group to see at once.

Read one or two chapters from one of the books. All are very readable, but *Runaway Ralph* is especially appealing to read aloud.

Describe how to locate the books in the fiction collection by writing the call numbers on the chalkboard and demonstrating where the books would be shelved. Encourage the children to borrow and to read the books on their own. There will not be enough copies for each child in the class to read a book by the same author at once. Assist the other children in finding other interesting books that they are able to read.

Follow-up: After the children have read the book, provide the opportunity for them to share some of the things that they liked with the rest of the children in the class. You may want to set up a simple reserve system for circulating the more popular books.

Variation: You may want to read from the same book for several sessions and possibly read an entire book to give the children an understanding of the full sweep of a sustained fictional work. This will help to motivate children to stick with a book until they have read it to the end.

Some other authors to introduce are:

Carolyn Haywood
Roald Dahl
Michael Bond
E. B. White
Astrid Lindgren

II. INTERPRETATION SKILLS   B. Parts of a Book

CREATE YOUR OWN BOOK

Children write and compile their own books in this activity, which provides them with an opportunity to review all the various parts of a book learned in the first, second, and third grades. It also provides a satisfying, creative experience for the children to become authors and to produce a finished product.

Time: Eight 30-minute sessions
Materials: White unlined paper, 9″ × 12″—5 to 6 sheets per child
Colored construction paper, 9″ × 12″—1 sheet per child
Lined writing paper—2 or 3 sheets per child
Pencils
Crayons
Rulers

Preparation: The children should be able to identify the following parts of a book: table of contents, dedication, preface, glossary, cover, title page, title, author, illustrator, publisher, copyright data.

Activity Directions:
Sessions I and II—Have the children write a story that they would like to share with younger children. You may wish to have some story starters around

the room for those children who need ideas. One type of story starter for this age is pictures that show action. Good sources of pictures of this type are covers of children's magazines and illustrations in picture books. Be certain that the children understand that they may use their own ideas and that they are not required to use an idea from a story starter. You may wish to suggest beginnings, such as "It all began early on a sunny, summer morning ..."

> **NOTE:** *An overabundance of suggestions may inhibit individual creativity at this age. The directions should allow the children to have a wide range of modes and subjects to choose from for their stories.*
>
> *Some children may wish to write nonfiction books, such as* How to Make a Pizza *or* My Dog Tuffy, *while others may write a fantasy, and still others a humorous nonsense story. You may find it more effective to individually assist those students who are experiencing difficulty getting started.*

Allow for a period of pre-writing. Time is needed to collect thoughts and to plan how to proceed before writing can begin. Most of the children should start writing after 5 to 10 minutes. The stories will take two 30-minute sessions to write. Proofread to correct spelling errors and other mistakes.

Session III—Give each child two sheets of 9″ × 12″ white unlined paper. After demonstrating the procedure, have the children fold the paper in half and place one sheet inside the other. Have the children number the pages from one to eight. Next, have the children draw lines on the bottom half of each page by using a ruler to measure 5 inches down from the top. Have the children put a dot at the 5-, 6-, 7-, and 8-inch sections of the page and draw horizontal lines at these points using the ruler. Then have them copy their stories into the book using the lines as guidelines. Encourage them to print as neatly as possible, leaving the top of each page free for a picture.

Warn them to plan the placement of their illustrations before copying the story so that the pages will be spaced properly.

Session IV—Have the children draw and color a picture on the top half of each page to illustrate the story.

> **NOTE:** *The children may need an extra session to complete their books up to this point.*

Session V—Give each child a piece of white unlined paper. Explain to the children that they are going to make a title page for their books. Have them fold the paper in half and slip it on the outside of their books. Say, "At the top, write the title of your book. Next, write 'Written and Illustrated by' and your name." Write "Written and Illustrated by" on the chalkboard or a chart. Explain that the bottom of the title page is the place where the name of the publishing company appears, and briefly review the fact that the publisher prints, compiles, and distributes the book. Have the children use the name of the school library media center for the publisher.

Say, "On the back of the title page, in the center, write a C with a circle around it and this year's date. This is the date of publication or the copyright date." Discuss copyright briefly: "Copyright means that this is your work and no one can use it without your permission."

Next, have the children turn to the back of their book and write "Glossary" at the top of the page. Discuss the likenesses of a glossary and a dictionary. Have the children find two to four words in their story that they think a younger child might not understand. Direct them to write those words and their meanings in the glossary, or have them write another word that has a similar meaning, or have them follow both of these exercises.

Session VI—Give the children a piece of white unlined paper to be folded as usual and placed on the outside of the book and inside the title page. The title page should be on the outside.

Discuss the use of a table of contents. Explain that, if a book has chapters, the table of contents lists the titles of the chapters and the pages. Have the children whose books have chapters make a table of contents.

Next, discuss the use of an index and the difference between a table of contents and an index. Have all of the children find two to five words in their book to list in an index. These words should be listed on the blank page at the end of their book. Have the children write "Index" at the top of the page and print each word with the page on which the word may be found.

Write the word *dedication* on the chalkboard. Read several dedications from books in the library media center. Have the children think of someone to whom they want to dedicate their book. On the back of the table of contents or, if a table of contents was not included, on the blank page intended for the table of contents, have the children write the names of the people to whom they are dedicating their book.

Next comes the final step in the project: designing the cover. Let each child select the color of the construction paper and fold it in half. Have the children place the cover on the outside of the book. They will need to write the title of their book and the word *by*, followed by their own name. They may decorate their covers if they wish. Staple the covers along the fold, making certain all of the pages are within the staples.

Sessions VII and VIII—Have a read-around and display the books in the library media center. The children may want to read their books to other younger classes or circulate them with the library media center collection.

Follow-up: You may wish to bind the books and include them in the library media center collection. A simple binding procedure is to paste cardboard on the inside of the front and the back covers and to place a strip of masking tape along the outside spine of the book. There are other, more complicated and sturdier bookbinding techniques that you might wish to use.

A spine label may be attached to the book and it may be given a call number and placed with the regular collection, or the books may be shelved together as a special collection.

II. INTERPRETATION SKILLS   C. Research and Reporting Techniques

RESEARCH AND REPORT

This activity provides an opportunity to locate information on a topic in an encyclopedia and to report on the information. It also helps children to learn that an encyclopedia is a source of information on people, places, and things. The activity requires that the children recall, summarize, and paraphrase the information that they find and to report on it through writing and drawing.

Time: Four 30-minute sessions

Materials: Encyclopedias from the library media center collection
Lined writing paper
Drawing paper, 12″ × 18″
Pencils
Crayons

Activity Directions:

Session I—Explain to the children that the library media center is a good place to find out about some things that are interesting to them. Ask them to think of some things that they enjoy learning about and would like to know more about. Encourage the children to name the topics. List the topics on a chalkboard or chart. Broad subject areas, such as horses, dogs, California, soccer, football, and George Washington, may be listed. It is not necessary for the children to narrow their topics at this stage.

Explain that encyclopedias are a good source of information on the topics. Write "PEOPLE," "PLACES," and "THINGS" at the top of the list of topics. Explain that encyclopedias have information on people, places, and things. Have the children fit the topics on the list into one of the three categories.

Have the children choose one of the topics from the list so they can learn more about it. Ask how they will find the topic in an encyclopedia. Choose several children to explain the way to locate encyclopedia articles. Develop the understanding that the topics in encyclopedias are arranged alphabetically. Have each child name his or her topic and the volume of the encyclopedia in which they expect to find the topic.

Direct the children to select the appropriate encyclopedia volume from the reference collection and to sit at a table and find an article on their topic. Assist children who experience difficulty.

Allow approximately 10 minutes for the children to scan the articles on their topics. Draw attention to the different ways information is presented, such as pictures, charts, and maps.

Have the children return the encyclopedias to the proper place in the reference collection. Remind them to remember their topics, which they will continue to research in the next session.

Session II—Briefly review how to locate information in encyclopedias by having several children explain the process. Have the children relocate the encyclopedia volume that they used in the previous session and sit at a table with the volume.

Direct the children to read about their topics. Explain that while they read they should think about things that are especially interesting and that they would like to remember.

Allow 10 to 15 minutes for them to read the articles. Have the children close the encyclopedias and return them to their proper places in the reference collection. Some children may need more time to read their articles. Provide extra time if it is needed.

Pass around paper and pencils and ask the children to write about the topics from memory. Explain that they may write whatever they recalled from the encyclopedia. Writing about a topic while the encyclopedia is opened may tempt them to copy.

Have the children write two or three paragraphs, or approximately one page, about their topics. Assist children individually with spelling and other difficulties.

Session III—Return the papers to the children and give them an opportunity to rewrite their reports. Assist the children who need help.

Staple the reports to the lower half of drawing paper. Have the children illustrate their reports in the space on the drawing paper above the report.

Session IV—Have each child read his or her writing and show the picture to the rest of the children. After each reading, provide an opportunity for discussion and questions on the topic.

Follow-up: Display the reports on a bulletin board in the library media center, near the reference collection if possible. You might use the caption, "Encyclopedias Tell About People, Places, and Things."

II. INTERPRETATION SKILLS   D. Listening and Viewing Skills

STORY EXTENSION

This activity helps children to understand and to interpret what they see and hear. The activity provides an opportunity for children to extend a story using their own ideas.

Time: Four 30-minute sessions

Materials: *The Abominable Swamp Man* by Gail Haley.
New York: The Viking Press, 1975.

Paper
Pencils
Crayons

Activity Directions:

Session I—Gather the children around for a story. Before beginning the story, ask the children to notice how the story changes. Read the first half of the story. Draw the children's attention to the realistic beginning of the story and the way it gradually changes into a fantasy. Have the children describe the parts of the story that are realistic and the parts that are fantasy.

Session II—Have the children recall, summarize, and paraphrase the first half of the story. Finish reading the story. After the story, explain that the ending leaves some unanswered questions. Have the children discuss what they think are the unanswered questions. Develop the understanding that Edwardina used only one of her three wishes. Ask the children to think about how they would have Edwardina use the other two wishes.

Session III—Have several children recall, summarize, and paraphrase the story. Explain that the story ended leaving Edwardina with two unused wishes. Have the children write and illustrate extensions to the story that tell how Edwardina would use the two remaining wishes.

Session IV—Have a read-around in which the children share their story extensions with the rest of the class. Let each child have a turn to read his or her story and to show the picture.

Follow-up: The story extensions may be displayed on a bulletin board.

Variations: This activity may be adapted to other stories. Choose stories with open-ended conclusions that may be extended by the children.

V. FOURTH GRADE

Using the Library Media Center Independently

In the fourth grade, the children increase their ability to use the library media center independently. They become familiar with the wide range of materials in the library media center and locate and use the materials with a minimum of assistance from the library media specialist.

This chapter provides:

- A description of fourth graders' needs in terms of the library program
- A checklist of library skills to be developed at the fourth level
- Activities for teaching specific skills

THE FOURTH GRADE PROGRAM

The Card Catalog

If the children are to find materials on their own, they have to be able to use the card catalog effectively. This requires that they be able to alphabetize by interior letters, to use subject headings, and to know that materials may be located by author, title, and subject.

Alphabetizing

By the fourth grade, many children have acquired the skill of alphabetizing by interior letters. Alphabetizing in this way requires concentration. They may easily become distracted and confused. At these times a word of encouragement from you and a gentle urging to try again, along with some timely assistance, will build self-confidence while developing competence. Children's attitudes about using the library develop with the experiences they encounter in the early stages of library media center use. If they are given the impression that locating materials is so simple that only a fool would have difficulty, they will be embarrassed about experiencing problems and will avoid using the library. On the other hand, if they learn at the initial stage that the library media center materials are sometimes difficult to find, but are well worth the effort, they will be more likely to continue to develop independence and confidence.

Subject Headings

Fourth graders usually request library media center materials by subject. They often have difficulty locating these materials. The term that the child uses may not be the term used in the card catalog. Children naturally think that every term is in the card catalog. They often interpret not finding a card on a topic as an indication that there is no material to be found in the library media center on that topic. Cross-references are helpful in these cases, but there are few cross-references in the card catalog in relation to all of the possible terms the children might use.

The children need to learn to think of synonyms for their topics. They need to use alternative terms that would be appropriate subject headings. The activity "What's the Subject?" on page 104, provides practice in thinking of alternative terms that are appropriate subject headings. After the children have tried several alternative terms, however, encourage them to ask you to suggest a subject heading. It is important for them to learn when to ask for the help of a librarian and when to continue on their own.

Author, Title, and Subject Cards

In the fourth grade, the children learn that they may look up books in the card catalog by the author or title as well as the subject. This type of access to materials is simpler and more straightforward than subject access.

It is helpful for the children to be aware of when they need to use author and title cards. Have them think of times when they might look up a book in these ways. For example, if they have read a fiction book that they especially liked, they might want to know if the library media center has other books by the same author; if they know the title of a fiction book but not the author, they will need the author's name or the call number to locate the book on the shelf.

Dewey Decimal System

After the children have found the card in the catalog and have made a note of the call number, they need a general idea of what the number means in order to locate the material. At this point it is important that they become familiar with the organization of the Dewey Decimal System.

If fourth graders know the ten main classes of the Dewey Decimal System and where each is located in the library media center, they can go to the appropriate section and locate the materials. At this time, most children are not ready to learn how each class is divided and subdivided or the function of the decimal point. They can understand that all nonfiction materials are divided into 10 general categories and that each category is a separate area of human endeavor and knowledge.

You can explain each of the 10 categories in simple terms for the children to understand. Although they are not required to memorize each category, they should have a general understanding of the subject covered in the divisions and of the location where corresponding materials could be found in the library media center. For example, it is not necessary to know that 500 is science, but it will be helpful for the children to know that there is a section of science materials and to have a general idea where the science section is located.

Research and Reporting Techniques

Nine-year-old children continue in a period of slow, steady growth. They are capable of extended periods of close attention and prolonged interest. An increasing number of individual differences appear, and there is a wide range of reading and writing ability. At this age, children often show rapid development in the ability to initiate and complete tasks.

Fourth graders use the library media center to gather information for the subjects they are studying in school. They need opportunities to apply their abilities in the communication skills of reading, writing, listening, and speaking to learning in subject areas. Assignments should allow for the wide range of abilities of individual children. Tasks may be structured so that all of the children may be genuinely interested and successful, whatever their level of reading and writing may be.

The library media center is especially suited to providing interesting tasks within a wide range of capabilities. The children can get a broad sweeping overview of a topic or delve deeply into the details of a subject. Research and reporting for subject areas can be sufficiently flexible to accommodate each child's interest and capability.

Coordinating with
the Subject Areas of the Curriculum

Careful planning with the teacher of the subject areas is necessary. The teacher needs to know possible research and reporting opportunities that the library media center offers. The library media specialist needs to know the topics that are to be covered and the general abilities of the children in a particular class.

Coordinating the library media center program with the instruction in various areas of the curriculum is not an easy task. There are seldom any formal patterns of joint planning established. Although you intend to plan together on a consistent basis, limited time and work pressures all too often make informal attempts at planning unpredictable, inadequate, and disappointing.

For an effective library media center program, joint planning is essential. You cannot expect the children to learn how to use the library media center to research and report information without being required to put the skill to use in a meaningful way. The most effective time to instruct fourth graders in using encyclopedias is when they have been asked to gather information by a teacher and need to use the encyclopedia to accomplish the task.

The library media center offers a rich storehouse of materials that greatly enhance instruction in subject areas. The library media center can also accommodate the wide range of interests and abilities of the children, which is so often neglected in the instruction of subjects that use texts.

Coordination between the library media center program and subject instruction is well worth the effort for both the library media specialist and the classroom teacher. But the children are the ultimate beneficiaries of a well-coordinated program. They learn to use the materials in the library media center so they can gather information independently, following their own inclinations and interests. They begin to experience that learning is an individual, lifelong endeavor in which the library can play a central role.

Encyclopedias

One of the research and reporting techniques fourth graders learn is the use of an encyclopedia. An in-depth analysis of encyclopedias is provided in the six-session activity, "Exploring Encyclopedias," beginning on page 105. The children are introduced to the important features of encyclopedias and learn techniques to interpret the information presented. This analysis helps to provide a general understanding of reference sources and forms a basis for using other reference sources.

Indexes

Another research and reporting technique fourth graders need is the ability to use indexes in books to locate information on a topic. Often, when there is not an entire book in the nonfiction collection devoted to a certain topic, the children assume that the library media center does not have information on that topic. The activity "Look It Up," on page 111, provides the children with opportunities to locate information on topics within books using indexes. This useful research skill is easily overlooked by students.

Bibliography

At this early stage of learning techniques to gather information to report on a topic, it is important for children to understand that when they use someone's ideas they must give that person credit. Simplified bibliographic form is introduced. Noting the authors and the titles of books used for gathering information can become a natural part of reporting at this age.

Two-Source Research and Reporting

Combining information from several sources into a cohesive report is a very difficult skill. Nine-year-olds may begin developing this skill by using two sources for a report, usually an encyclopedia article and a book. Many children, however, will not be ready to combine even two sources. Those children should continue to use one source until they have had sufficient practice and are ready to branch out. Encourage most of the children to attempt using two sources by the end of the fourth grade.

Working in Groups

Many of the activities in this section are planned for small groups or partners. Children of this age enjoy their peers. They are cooperative and able to work together. Small groups provide opportunities for each child to participate in an activity. In large group activities, which include the entire class, only a few children may actively participate.

Children can often far exceed their individual capacity by working in a group. Small groups enable more capable children to assist less able children. Each child can contribute to the group according to his or her ability, interest, and experience.

Using the Library Media Center Collection

Fourth graders use a wide variety of library media center materials. In addition to fiction, nonfiction, and reference materials, they begin to make more consistent use of periodicals, biographies, and audiovisual materials.

Periodicals

The children, no longer limited to the primary periodicals, may read all of the magazines in the library media center collection. Many of the magazines appeal to personal interests that individual children have developed. Once a child is acquainted with the magazines pertaining to his or her area of interest, he or she will often follow the periodical, faithfully reading each new issue as it appears.

Biographies

Biographies are very appealing to fourth graders. Nine is the age when hero worship begins to emerge. The children enjoy reading about the lives of famous people they admire. They also show an interest in patriotism at this time and are interested in biographies of historical figures.

Audiovisual Materials

Many library media centers have extensive collections of audiovisual materials, including filmstrips, filmloops, records, videotapes, and cassettes. Fourth graders can use these materials on their own. The equipment is simple to operate and relatively sturdy. You can teach several children individually, and they can teach others who want to operate the equipment.

When the children are gathering information on a topic, they may also want to view a filmstrip or other audiovisual material on the topic. If the cards for audiovisual materials are interfiled in the card catalog, the children can easily determine what is available on their topic. The storage of audiovisual materials varies from one library media center to another. You may have a system in which the children can locate the materials on their own, or you may need to assist them in finding the materials. Set up a listening and viewing area in the library media center where they can use audiovisual materials individually and in small groups.

Reading

By the fourth grade, many children have experienced the pleasure of reading fiction and have favorite authors and books. Continue reading aloud to them. Choose books having lively, unpredictable stories that appeal to a broad range of individual tastes. Read the beginnings of books to stir children's interest and curiosity. Encourage them to continue reading individually to find out what happens. Occasionally read an entire book to provide all of the children with the experience of following a sustained reading of a story. Book talks, which describe several books on one theme or by one author, are an excellent way to introduce the children to new books and to entice them to read.

When a fourth grade class comes to the library media center, provide time for quiet reading after the children have selected books to borrow. In this way, the children become involved in the book before they leave the library media center. Once their interest is sparked, they will be more likely to continue reading on their own. This quiet reading time need be only 5 or 10 minutes, just time enough for the children to get into the first chapter of the book.

Book Logs

Independent reading is a solitary activity requiring that children isolate themselves from others. While this aspect of reading appeals to some children, it repels others. Nine-year-old children enjoy the company of others. They form strong attachments with one another, which frequently change, but are nonetheless very important to them. The activity "My Book Log," on page 111, has each child keep a log of the books from the library media center that he or she has read. The children regularly share what they read by exchanging and reading each other's logs. In this way the solitary nature of reading, which is undesirable to many nine-year-olds, is somewhat diminished.

The book log provides each child with an account of his or her personal reading over an extended time. The children easily forget what they have read. Keeping a log helps them to recall their reading. Don't require a detailed book report. Rather, encourage the children to write something that describes the book in a way that distinguishes it from others they have read. They can recall and summarize the book in their minds and then paraphrase by writing a brief description of the book in their own words. The book logs help them to evaluate books and to improve their ability to make satisfying reading selections.

Kinds of Fiction— Mystery and Fantasy

Fourth graders can understand that there are different kinds of fiction and that each kind has certain features. They may begin to develop a preference for one kind of fiction. The main emphasis in the fourth grade is on the unique characteristics of mystery and fantasy. The activity entitled "Mystery," on page 114, helps children deepen their understanding and appreciation of these kinds of literature. After reading mysteries and discussing the characteristics of mysteries, the children write their own mystery stories. By attempting to write within the confines of the particular form, the children come to a fuller understanding of that type of literature. In this way, they learn about this kind of fiction through their own experience.

Writing of this kind provides opportunities for the children to extend what they read. They use their own ideas to create a story using the features of a particular kind of fiction that they have read. Some of them will write stories that are replicas of what they have seen on television or recently read. Other stories will be highly original. The object of the activity is not to turn the children into authors, although that might occasionally be an added outcome. The object is to give all of them the opportunity to use the elements of mystery to write a story and to experience the literature first hand or from the inside.

When the children read mysteries thereafter, they may more fully appreciate the author's technique and talent. In this way, they will more fully understand this form of literature and develop the ability to evaluate and select what they read.

Television and Reading

An important aspect of the library media program is to help children to effectively use the information sources available to them. One of the main sources of information in the children's lives is television. Fourth graders need to become aware that as there are different types of materials in the library media center, there are also different types of programs on television. Some library media center materials are entertaining and others are informative. Some television programs are viewed for entertainment; others offer more informative material. It may be helpful to point out that television offers fiction and nonfiction materials, as the library media center does.

To fully understand and use the two types of television programming, the children need to be aware of the differences between fiction and nonfiction television. The kind of attention given to each of the two types of programming is different. While viewing fictional television, the child becomes involved in his or her feelings and flows along with little conscious effort. The experience during the time that the program is viewed is important. In nonfiction television, the child's attention must be more concentrated and directed to the central point and to the information given. The emphasis is on what is recalled after the program.

Early opportunities to become aware of these differences will enable children to use television more effectively. The activity entitled "The First Americans," on page 113, provides opportunities to recall, summarize, paraphrase, and extend information from nonfiction television.

These activities may also be practiced in more informal ways. For example, when the children are sharing their experiences about mysteries that they have read, they might tell about mysteries that they have seen on television or in film. At that time, you might ask them to describe the differences in viewing a mystery and reading a mystery. In this way, they have an opportunity to compare the experiences and to become aware of the differences.

Television and reading also have basic differences that the children can eventually understand. Television is viewed at a predetermined pace. The child cannot stop a program to reflect on a certain point or speed up an uninteresting portion, although this may be possible to a limited extent with a videotape. In reading, the reader adjusts the pace to the type of material being read. The child can choose to read faster than he or she talks, slow down to think over a point, or skim less significant sections. In this way, reading may be made compatible with an individual's thought. There are many other differences that might be pointed out. If you begin to compare the two types of media, the children will offer many suggestions of their own.

One further point about television and reading: *The two types of media are not in competition with each other.* Each provides a different, but compatible experience. Television can lead to reading, and reading can lead to an interest in a television program. When *The Lion, the Witch, and the Wardrobe,* by C.S. Lewis, was shown on television, the children who had read the book looked forward to seeing the program. After the program was aired, there was a great demand for the book (Macmillan, 1970) by children whose interest was sparked.

There is one way the two modes are in competition, however. Each mode competes for the child's time. Through the library media center program, children may be helped to make better decisions on how to spend their time and on how to make more intelligent media choices.

Summary

In the fourth grade, the children develop the ability to find and use materials independently. They apply their communication skills of reading, writing, listening, and speaking to learning. The children begin to use the library media center to research and report on topics in subject areas of the curriculum. They become more able to evaluate and to select materials for information and enjoyment.

FOURTH GRADE LIBRARY SKILLS
CHECKLIST AND ACTIVITIES

The following presents a sequential checklist of library and information skills to be developed at the fourth grade level and suggested activities for teaching specific skills. Each activity is keyed to a major skill objective at the fourth level and is ready for your immediate use or adaptation.

Library Skills Checklist
FOURTH GRADE

Class_____

I. Location Skills
A. Card Catalog
1. Understands that the card catalog is an index to the library media center collection
2. Can locate materials using call numbers on catalog cards
3. Can use the card catalog to locate materials by author, title, and subject

   a. **Alphabetizing**
   (1) Can alphabetize by interior letters of words
   (2) Can interpret drawer labels on the card catalog

   b. **Subject Headings**
   (1) Can convert own terminology into that used in subject headings
   (2) Can be specific when looking up a subject

   c. **Descriptive Information**
   (1) Can interpret information on catalog cards, e.g., type of material, level of material, how recently published, whether illustrated
   (2) Can use information on catalog cards to compile a simple bibliography

B. Fiction and Nonfiction
1. Understands the difference between fiction and nonfiction
2. Knows that fiction and nonfiction are two main categories of library media center materials

C. Dewey Decimal System
1. Understands that the purpose of the Dewey Decimal System is to pull together materials on the same subject and literary form
2. Can locate materials using call numbers
3. Is acquainted with the ten main classes

D. Reference Collection
1. Knows reference sources are meant to be referred to, not read all the way through
2. Can locate information in reference sources

   a. **Encyclopedias**
   (1) Can use an encyclopedia for answering questions, for background information, and as a starting point for research
   (2) Can use an encyclopedia for an overview of a topic
   (3) Is familiar with the alphabetical arrangement of an encyclopedia and able to locate information with a minimum of assistance
   (4) Knows encyclopedias are a source of study guides, charts, maps, drawings, photographs, diagrams, graphs, and bibliographies
   (5) Can use the index in the encyclopedia to locate information on a specific topic
   (6) Can use the special-subject encyclopedias in the reference collection

Class_____

        b. **Dictionaries**
           (1) Can obtain definitions from dictionary entries
           (2) Can use alphabetical order and guide words in dictionary work
           (3) Knows there are specialized English language dictionaries

        c. **Other Reference Tools**
           (1) Knows the atlas is a book of maps
           (2) Knows the almanac is a source of statistics and other current facts

E. Biographical Sources
    1. Can define biography
    2. Can locate information about a person

F. Periodicals
    1. Is familiar with the intermediate magazines in the library media center
    2. Can use the intermediate magazines, both general and special-subject, for information and pleasure reading

G. Indexes
    1. Understands that any book may be used as a reference book if it has an index
    2. Can locate information on a subject using an index
    3. Can use indexes to find information when there is no complete book devoted to the topic in the library media center
    4. Can locate information in encyclopedias using indexes

H. Vertical Files
    1. Knows the type of materials found in a vertical file, e.g., pictures, clippings, pamphlets, maps
    2. Knows vertical file materials are not in the card catalog

I. Audiovisual Materials and Equipment
    1. Knows information comes in a variety of formats
    2. Can locate materials on a subject in the audiovisual materials collection with some assistance
    3. Can operate equipment in order to use the materials

Class_____

II. Interpretation Skills

A. Evaluation and Selection Techniques

1. Understands various forms of literature
2. Can select materials with a specific purpose in mind
3. Is acquainted with authors and their works
4. Begins to evaluate a book for quality

B. Parts of a Book

1. Can use the parts of a book to determine scope, format, and timeliness
2. Can use the parts of a book to locate and document information

C. Research and Reporting Techniques

1. Can research a topic using more than one source and compile findings into a report for presentation
2. Knows what a bibliography is and what purpose it serves
3. Can make a simple bibliography of author and title for all research assigned

D. Listening and Viewing Skills

1. Attends to the sights and sounds of the instructional situation
2. Interprets and understands what is heard and seen
3. Can recall, summarize, and paraphrase what is listened to and viewed

E. Literature Appreciation

1. Is familiar with various forms of literature
2. Can interpret meaning from literature and relate it to past experience

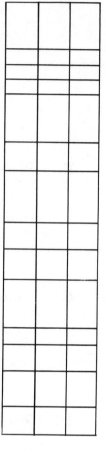

I. LOCATION SKILLS   A. Card Catalog

CALL NUMBERS

This activity provides an opportunity for children to become familiar with call numbers. It also prepares them to use call numbers to locate materials.

Time: 30 minutes

Materials: Paper
                  Pencils

Activity Directions:

Through an introductory discussion, define what a call number is, why it is used, and where it is found. Encourage the children to cite examples from their experiences in using the card catalog.

Explain that call numbers include both numbers and letters. Write the following on the chalkboard:

F   B   REF   796.1
AND   LIN   920   RUS

Have the children write down the section of the library media center where they would find each of these call numbers.

After the children have completed the task, collect the papers. Discuss the correct answers and write the corresponding section of the library media center collection under each call number.

Fiction   Biography   Reference   Nonfiction

Follow-up: Return the papers in the next session. Have the children correct their mistakes.

I. LOCATION SKILLS   A. Card Catalog

THREE-CARD SEARCH

This activity provides practice in using the card catalog to locate materials by author, title, and subject.

Time: 30 minutes

Materials: Books from the nonfiction collection
                  Paper
                  Pencils

Preparation: Select a nonfiction book for half of the children in the class. Choose books that have obvious subject headings such as BIRDS, DOGS, BASEBALL.

Activity Directions:

Explain that there are three ways to look up a book in the card catalog. Write "AUTHOR," "TITLE," and "SUBJECT" on the chalkboard. Have the children choose a partner and find the three types of cards in the card catalog for the book given to them. Tell them to copy the first line of each card just as it is printed on the card.

Allow 15 to 20 minutes for completion of the activity. Remind the children to take turns at the card catalog. You may want them to take the drawers back to their tables to avoid congestion and to return them as soon as they are finished to give someone else a turn to use the drawer.

Have the children report back to the class on what they found. Have each group read the first line of each card and identify whether it is a title, author, or subject card. Draw attention to the fact that subject headings are printed in capital letters. Have the children observe that the author's last name appears first, followed by a comma and the first name.

I. LOCATION SKILLS   A. Card Catalog

USING DRAWER LABELS

This worksheet activity provides practice alphabetizing by interior letters of words. The exercise also gives children opportunities to interpret alphabetical arrangement of the drawer labels of the card catalog.

Time: 30 minutes

Materials: Worksheet for each child in the class (see page 103)
                 Pencils

Preparation: Duplicate worksheets. Copy the drawer labels from the card catalog in your library media center.

Activity Directions:

Have the children do the following worksheet. Read and discuss the directions to assure that each child understands what he or she is to do. Allow about 20 minutes to complete the exercise. Assist children individually who are experiencing difficulty. Collect the worksheets at the end of the session.

Follow-up: In a subsequent session, correct and discuss the worksheet. Give the children opportunities to ask questions on any point that they don't understand. Repeat the exercise using other books if more practice is needed.

Name:_____ Date:_____

USING THE DRAWER LABELS ON THE CARD CATALOG

A-AQ	D	I	N	SN-SZ
AR-AZ	E	J	O	T
B-BH	F-FH	K	P	U-V
BI-BZ	FI-FZ	L	Q	W
C-CH	G	M-ME	R	X-Y
CI-CZ	H	MF-MZ	S-SM	Z

In which drawer of the card catalog would you locate a card for these books? Write the drawer label in the space following each book.

1. A book by Beverly Cleary _____

2. A book about bats _____

3. A book about automobiles _____

4. *Mystery of the Fat Cat* _____

5. Andersen's Fairy Tales _____

6. *Soccer Halfback* _____

7. A book about fishing _____

8. A book by Margery Sharp _____

9. A book about Canada _____

10. A book by Eleanor Cameron _____

I. LOCATION SKILLS   A. Card Catalog

WHAT'S THE SUBJECT?

This activity provides practice in converting the child's terminology into that used in subject headings. It also requires the children to be specific when looking up a subject.

Time: 30 minutes

Materials: Paper
                 Pencils

Preparation: Write the following on a chalkboard:

> Cars
> Trains
> Planes
> Farming
> Jokes

Activity Directions:

Explain that if someone wanted information on the topics listed above, he or she might have difficulty finding it in the card catalog. These are not subject headings that are used in the card catalog. Have the children think of other terms that have the same meaning that might be a subject heading used in the card catalog. Explain that they may use the card catalog for help.

Divide the class into groups of two or three to work together to find alternative terms. Allow 15 minutes for completion of the task. Have the children report the appropriate subject headings and describe how they found them. Write the correct subject heading on the chalkboard after each term:

> Automobiles
> Railroads
> Airplane
> Agriculture
> Humor

Variation: This exercise may be put on a ditto to be completed by the children individually. You may repeat this activity using other terms.

I. LOCATION SKILLS   C. Dewey Decimal System

CATEGORIES

This class activity helps students understand that the purpose of the Dewey Decimal System is to pull together materials on the same subject and literary form. It involves children in locating materials using call numbers and acquaints them with the 10 main classes.

Time: Three 30-minute sessions
Materials: Construction paper
                   Scissors
                   Discarded magazines
                   Paste
Activity Directions:
Session I—Divide the class into 10 groups, assign a Dewey Decimal category to each group, and give them the name of their category, such as 100 Philosophy, 200 Religion, or 300 Social Sciences. Direct the groups to find a dictionary definition for their category and several examples of topics covered within their category.

Allow 10 or 15 minutes for the groups to gather the information, and have each group report back to the class.

Session II—Have the class assemble in the 10 groups and distribute the materials listed above to each group. Invite each group to make a poster illustrating their category by clipping pictures from magazines and mounting them on the construction paper.

Session III—Direct one group to hold up their poster and to challenge another group to find materials from that category. Record the time it takes to locate the materials. Continue until all groups have had a turn.

The group with the shortest time is the winner.

Follow-up: Display the posters near the corresponding sections of your library media center collection.

I. LOCATION SKILLS   D. Reference Collection

(1) EXPLORING ENCYCLOPEDIAS

This multi-session activity helps children understand the alphabetical arrangement of an encyclopedia and provides practice in locating information on topics.

Time: 30 minutes
Materials: A volume of an encyclopedia for each child in the class
Activity Directions:
Have the children describe the kind of topics found in the encyclopedia. List the topics on the chalkboard as the children name them. Write "People," "Places," and "Things" at the top of the list. Ask the children to identify the topics that belong in each category. Explain that encyclopedias have information on people, places, and things (which include events).

Give each child a volume of an encyclopedia. Allow a few minutes for browsing through the encyclopedia. While the children are browsing, ask them to notice the aids that will help them to find a certain topic. Lead the children in a brief discussion of the alphabetical arrangement of the topics and the use of guide words.

Have the children find information on an animal in their encyclopedia. Allow five minutes to locate the topic and skim the article. Have each child share with the class how he or she found the topic and one or two interesting facts about the animal.

(2) ENCYCLOPEDIAS

In this session, children learn to use an encyclopedia for an overview of a topic by becoming familiar with the use of headings and subheadings.

Time: 30 minutes

Materials: Reprint of the same encyclopedia article for each child in the class. Classroom copies of encyclopedia reprints are available at a nominal cost from World Book. Write:

> World Book, Inc.
> Box 3565
> Chicago, Illinois 60654

Paper

Pencils

Activity Directions:

Give each child a reprint of the same article from an encyclopedia. Write "Heading" and "Subheading" on the chalkboard. Have the children give several examples of headings from the article. Next, have them name several subheadings under each heading. Lead the children in a discussion of why headings and subheadings are used. Have them consider the difference in reading the information without the use of these captions.

Have the children list the headings on a piece of paper, leaving ample space after each one. Next, have the children indent an inch and under each heading list the subheadings. When all have completed the lists, have the children number the headings with Roman numerals and the subheadings with letters under each heading. Point out that they now have an outline of the topic. Allow 10 minutes for completion of the task and assist those children experiencing difficulty. Any child who finishes quickly may assist others needing help.

Have several children name the headings and subheadings that they found while the others correct any errors that they have made.

(3) ENCYCLOPEDIAS

This session enables children to learn that encyclopedias are a source of charts, maps, drawings, photographs, diagrams, graphs, study guides, and bibliographies.

Time: 30 minutes

Materials: Reprint of the same encyclopedia article for each child in the class

Write: World Book—Childcraft International, Inc.
          Box 3565
          Chicago, Illinois 60654

Paper
Pencils

Activity Directions:

Give each child a reprint of the same encyclopedia article, a piece of paper, and a pencil. Ask the children to browse through the article, looking for six different kinds of illustrations. Have them list the kinds of illustrations and the page numbers on which they are found. Allow 5 to 10 minutes to complete the lists.

Have the children share what they found, giving examples of each kind of illustration. On the chalkboard, list the kinds of illustrations as they are named.

Draw attention to the labels and captions under each illustration. Have several children read examples while the others follow in their articles.

Have the children turn to the last page of the article. Give a few minutes so they can scan the study guide and the bibliography. Lead the class in a brief discussion about the use of each of these aids.

(4) ENCYCLOPEDIAS

This activity enables children to locate and to interpret information in an encyclopedia with a minimum of assistance. It acquaints children with the format of encyclopedia articles that use a lead sentence followed by the body of the article.

Time: 30 minutes

Materials: Encyclopedias

Activity Directions:

Have the children form groups of three or four. Give each group an encyclopedia. Explain that each encyclopedia article has a lead and a body. The lead gives a brief definition of the topic, similar to that found in a dictionary. The first sentence of an article is the lead. The body follows the lead and gives more detailed facts about the topic.

Have the children select in their encyclopedia an article on an animal. Direct them to read the lead and scan the article for several details to share with the class. Allow 10 to 15 minutes to complete this assignment.

Have one child in each group read the lead to the class and have the other members of the group name a detail from the body.

(5) ENCYCLOPEDIAS

This session helps children use the index in the encyclopedia to locate information on a specific topic.

Time: 30 minutes
Materials: Indexes from several encyclopedias:

The World Book Encyclopedia.
Chicago: World Book—Childcraft International, Inc.

Compton's Encyclopedia.
Chicago: F. E. Compton Co.

The New Book of Knowledge.
New York: Grolier, Inc.

Encyclopedia International.
New York: Grolier, Inc.

Britannica Junior Encyclopedia.
Chicago: Encyclopedia Britannica, Inc.

Preparation: List the names of various animals on the chalkboard.
Activity Directions:
Have the children recall when they have used indexes in books. Ask them to describe when they might need an encyclopedia index. Through a brief discussion, point out that an index is used when a person can't find information on a topic under the alphabetical arrangement of the encyclopedia or when a person wants additional information.

Divide the children into groups of three or four. Give each group an encyclopedia index. Have them find the answers to the following questions:

1. How is the index arranged?
2. How would you find information from the citation given, for example, Africa A:100?

After approximately five minutes, have each group report to the class the answers in relation to their index.

Have the children choose an animal from those listed on the chalkboard and find information on it in a volume of the encyclopedia other than the one containing the beginning letter of the name of the animal. Allow 10 to 15 minutes for the children to complete the task. Assist groups that are experiencing difficulty. Have each group report the procedure they followed and the information they found to the class. Have them show the other groups both the citation in the index and the information in the volume of the encyclopedia.

(6) ENCYCLOPEDIAS

This session helps children to become acquainted with the special subject encyclopedias in the reference collection.
Time: 30 minutes
Materials: Special subject encyclopedias:

The Book of Popular Science.
New York: Grolier, Inc.

The Illustrated Animal Kingdom.
New York: Grolier, Inc.

Lands and People.
New York: Grolier, Inc.

The Lincoln Library of Sports Champions.
Columbus, Ohio: Frontier Press.
Paper
Pencils

Activity Directions:
Divide the class into groups of three or four. Assign an encyclopedia to each group. Have them find the answers to the following questions:

1. What kind of information is in the encyclopedia?
2. How would you find information on a topic?

Allow 15 minutes to investigate the encyclopedias. Assist any groups that are having difficulty.

Have the children in each group report to the class what they found out about the encyclopedia. Have them give specific examples from the encyclopedias.

Follow-up: When the children have completed the unit on using encyclopedias, they will need opportunities to practice what they have learned. Assignments from subject areas, such as social studies or science, that call for these abilities may be coordinated with this instruction.

I. LOCATION SKILLS   E. Biographical Sources

WHO IS THE SUBJECT?

This activity acquaints children with the various types of biographical sources in the library media center. It provides opportunities to locate information about a person and encourages children to read biographies.

Time: 30 minutes
Materials: Biographical sources on Abraham Lincoln from the library
                 media center collection
Preparation: Select 8 to 10 biographies of Abraham Lincoln, including materials in encyclopedias, biographical dictionaries, collective biographies, and biographies.

Activity Directions:
Have the children discuss the definition of *biography.* Choose several children to explain how to find a biography in the library media center. Ask them why they don't need to go to the card catalog to find a biography. Draw attention to the fact that the call number of a biography is based on the subject's last name. Compare call numbers of fictional works, which are based on the author's last name. Demonstrate the differences by writing examples of the two kinds of call numbers on the chalkboard.

Explain that there are different kinds of biographies in the library media center. If we wanted to know about a person's whole life in detail, we would find an entire book on that person. Sometimes we want to know only what the person was famous for. Have the children name some sources that are used to find summarized information about a person. Develop the understanding that encyclopedias have information about people. Describe other reference books that give information about famous people, such as biographical dictionaries.

Explain that collective biographies give information about the lives of a group of people with something in common. Draw attention to the location of the collective biographies in the library media center.

Divide the class into groups of three or four. Give each group a biography on Abraham Lincoln. Allow 10 minutes for the children to scan and to discuss the biography. Have each group describe the biography by explaining whether it is an entire book on one person, a book about several people, or a reference book with biographical information. Encourage them to point out where the biography is located in the library media center and to give several interesting facts that they found about Lincoln's life.

Follow-up: Encourage the children to borrow and to read biographies and to use the reference biographical sources.

I. LOCATION SKILLS   F. Periodicals

MAGAZINE COLLECTION

This activity helps children to become familiar with the magazine collection. It provides an opportunity for them to read magazines for pleasure or for information.

Time: 30 minutes
Materials: The magazine collection in the library media center
Activity Directions:
Select the latest issues of the magazines with which you think most of the children might not be familiar. Hold up each magazine and briefly describe its contents and format, showing several illustrations. Draw attention to the special emphasis in each magazine, such as sports, animal life, people around the world, or cars.

Have the children browse through the magazine collection, sampling its variety. Encourage them to borrow a magazine to read.

NOTE: *The circulation of magazines is handled in many different ways. Some library media specialists prefer not to circulate magazines, but to have them read in the library media center. For this activity, make an exception to the circulation policy so that the children can borrow magazines for a short time, enabling them to become more familiar with the magazines available to them.*

Follow-up: This activity may be repeated occasionally throughout the year.

I. LOCATION SKILLS   G. Indexes

LOOK IT UP

This activity helps children to understand that any book may be used as a reference book if it has an index. It provides opportunities for them to practice locating information on a topic using an index in a book.

Time: 30 minutes

Materials: Paper

Pencils

12 to 15 indexed nonfiction books on animals

Activity Directions:

Have the children work with partners. Give each pair a piece of paper and a book with an index. Ask the children to describe what they would do if they were looking for information on an animal but the library media center didn't have an entire book devoted to the topic.

Next, choose several children to explain the difference between an index and a table of contents. Help them understand that a table of contents lists chapter titles, whereas an index lists the various topics in the book and the pages on which they are found. The table of contents is in the front, and the index is usually found in the back.

Tell the children to use the index in the book to find information on three animals of their choice. Have them write one sentence about each animal and the citation they found in the index. Have each pair of children share with the class what they found.

Follow-up: Collect the papers and check to see whether all of the children understand how to locate information in a book by using an index. Plan individual instruction for those who need additional help.

II. INTERPRETATION SKILLS   A. Evaluation and Selection Techniques

"MY BOOK LOG"

This activity helps children to become acquainted with various authors and their writing and to develop some personal favorites. It helps them to compare and to evaluate the books that they have read.

Time: Two 30-minute sessions and additional sessions throughout the school year

Materials: Notebooks—one for each child

Pencils

Activity Directions:

Have the children keep a log of the books that they read from the library media center collection.

Session I—Have the children prepare the book logs. Give each child a notebook. Have them write a title page on the first page of the notebook, including the title *My Book Log*, their names, and the date. Explain that it is difficult to remember the books that you read over a period of time. Tell them, "The book log helps you remember by keeping a record of your readings throughout the year."

Have the children record the books they read by title, author, and call number. Encourage them to write a short paragraph that says something about that particular book and no other. Have the children make one or two entries of books that they have read recently. If they haven't read any books that they want to record, suggest that they choose a book to read and record it by the next session.

Session II—Provide 10 minutes for the children to record books in their logs. Have the children share the books they have read by exchanging the book logs with classmates.

> **NOTE:** *You may want to keep the logs in the library media center or have the children keep them. If the children keep the logs, there is the possibility that they might be mislaid, but this does allow the children to log books on their own without being limited to the library media center sessions.*

Follow-up: Continue the logs throughout the year by providing an occasional session for writing and sharing. At the end of the school year, have the children make covers for their logs, and display them in the library media center. Return the book logs so the children can take them home. Encourage the children to keep their book logs to remind them of what they read in the fourth grade.

II. INTERPRETATION SKILLS   C. Research and Reporting Techniques

GIVE PROPER CREDIT

This activity acquaints the children with the purpose of a bibliography. It provides an opportunity for them to make a simple bibliography for a report that they have done.

Time: Two 30-minute sessions
Materials: Library media center collection
                 Paper
                 Pencils
Preparation: This lesson should be taught in conjunction with an assigned report in a subject area.
Activity Directions:
Session I—Ask the children to imagine that they have invented a new machine to heat homes without using expensive fuel. Have them describe how they would protect their idea so that no one would take it. Discuss the use of patents.

Next, ask the children to imagine that they are authors who have written a book. Have them discuss how they would protect their ideas from being taken by someone who would not give them credit. Discuss bibliographies. Write "Bibliography" on the chalkboard.

Ask the children if they have heard of plagiarism. Explain that plagiarism occurs when a person steals an author's work and presents it as his or her own. Explain that credit must be given to the author of the book from which you get your ideas. When a person wants to use the author's exact words, that person must use quotation marks.

On the chalkboard, demonstrate how to cite a book and an encyclopedia. Use a simplified bibliographic form with the author and title of a book or the article, title, and volume of an encyclopedia.

Have the children make a bibliography of an encyclopedia article and of a book that they are using for a report. Collect the bibliographies at the end of the session.

Session II—During the second session review the bibliographies individually with the children. Have them correct any errors.

Follow-up: Coordinate this activity with an assigned report in a subject area. When the reports are completed, you might make arrangements with the teacher to check the bibliographies for correct citations. Go over any mistakes with individual children.

II. INTERPRETATION SKILLS   D. Listening and Viewing Skills

"THE FIRST AMERICANS"

This activity provides opportunities to attend to the sights and sounds of an audiovisual presentation and to interpret what is seen and heard. It enables children to understand what they view and listen to through recalling, summarizing, paraphrasing, and extending.

Time: 40 minutes

Materials: *American Scrapbook,** WVIZ TV, Cleveland, Ohio: "The First Amercians."

Other nonfiction television programs may be substituted.

Preparation: This activity should be coordinated with a unit of study in social studies.

Activity Directions:

Ask a question prior to showing the program to concentrate the children's attention on certain aspects of the information contained in the program. While the children view the program they should consider what changes took place after the arrival of the ships in 1607. Show the television program, which is 15 minutes in length.

Have the children recall and describe what Indian life was like. List the characteristics of Indian life on a chalkboard. Next, have them name some

---

*Distributed by Great Plains National ITV Library, Box 80669, Lincoln, Nebraska 68501.

changes that took place after 1607. List the changes on the chalkboard beside the description of Indian life. Read both lists and discuss some of the causes of the changes.

Follow-up: The social studies teacher may continue to draw on the more detailed information in the program.

Encourage the children to read further about Indian life.

II. INTERPRETATION SKILLS   E. Literature Appreciation

MYSTERY

This activity acquaints the children with the various forms of literature. By giving them opportunities to read, to discuss, and to write different types of fiction, they can more fully understand and interpret what they read.

Time: Six 30-minute sessions

Materials: *Mystery of the Fat Cat* by Frank Bonham.
New York: E.P. Dutton, 1968. Pap., Dell: 1971.

Deadline for McGurk by E.W. Hildick.
New York: Macmillan Publishing Co., 1975.

Other mysteries from the fiction collection
One piece of oaktag, 24″ × 36″
Marking pens
Paper
Pencils

Preparation: Make a poster to be displayed in the library media center.

KINDS OF FICTION
Mystery
Fantasy
Science
Historical
Adventure
Sports
Realistic
Humorous

Activity Directions:

Session I—Have the children discuss the following questions: What is a mystery? How is a mystery different from other fiction? Develop the following ideas: A mystery has an unsolved crime, a victim, suspects, someone who investigates and solves the crime, and clues leading to a solution. Explain how a mystery is like a puzzle.

Ask the children to listen for these elements while you read a mystery. Begin reading one of the mysteries suggested or one of your choice. Read expressively to create an atmosphere of suspense and intrigue.

Session II—Continue to read the mystery. Encourage the children to choose mysteries from the collection to borrow and to read. You may wish to display some mysteries on a separate shelf or table to help the children in their selection.

Session III—Recall and discuss the story briefly. Have the children name the characteristics that distinguish a mystery from other kinds of fiction. Write the characteristics on the chalkboard as they are named. Have the children think about a story they would write using the characteristics. Allow 5 to 10 minutes for the children to gather in small groups to talk about and to share their ideas. This provides them with an opportunity to plan their stories and to gather ideas.

Session IV—Write the following characteristics of a mystery on the chalkboard or a chart:

1. Unsolved crime
2. Victim
3. Suspects
4. Someone to investigate and solve the crime
5. Clues leading to a solution

Have the children write a short mystery using these characteristics. Toward the end of the session, choose several children to read their stories to the class. This helps the children who are having difficulty to formulate ideas from the example of another child's work.

Session V—Have the children continue writing the stories. Help children who need some assistance, especially with spelling and clear phrasing.

Session VI—Have a read-around and sharing session. First, have the children exchange and read each other's mysteries and make suggestions about each other's spelling and word usage. Next, encourage each child to read his or her mystery to the class.

Follow-up: Several of the stories may be chosen by the class to be displayed on a bulletin board. These stories may be recopied and mounted on a black construction paper background with various mystery symbols. Some mystery books may be displayed along with a duplicated handout of a list of the mysteries in the fiction collection of the library media center.

Variations: Fantasy books may be used in this same way. First, read one aloud to the children. The following are excellent fantasies to read to fourth graders. You may substitute any others that you wish.

Stuart Little by E. B. White.
New York: Harper and Row, 1945.

The Rescuers by Margery Sharp.
Boston: Little Brown, 1959. (Pap., Dell, 1974.)

Next, encourage the children to borrow and to read fantasies from the fiction collection. Have the children discuss what is unique about fantasies and write their own fantasy short stories. Conclude the unit by having the children share their stories with their classmates.

VI. FIFTH GRADE

Gathering Information
in Content Areas

In the fifth grade, children make full use of materials in the library media center for information and entertainment. They analyze the Dewey Decimal System as one way of classifying materials and compare it to other ways of organizing information. Research and reporting on topics in subject areas of the curriculum become central to the library media program.

This chapter provides:

- A description of fifth graders' needs in terms of the library program
- A checklist of library skills to be developed at the fifth level
- Activities for teaching specific skills

THE FIFTH GRADE PROGRAM

The ten-year-old emerges from a rather smooth period of slow, steady growth to enter a time of rapid, uneven growth, which results in an awkward, unstable stage. This growth stage continues for the next four to five years until the child reaches maturity. Growth patterns vary widely during this period. Girls usually begin this growth as much as two years earlier than boys. Children at ten display a wide range of individual differences in both maturity and ability levels. In planning a library media center program for fifth graders, it is helpful to consider these characteristics. The library media center is well equipped to provide for varying abilities, levels of maturity, and different personal interests.

Coordination

As the children progress through the elementary school, it becomes more important each year for the library media center program to be coordinated with subject instruction and learning. If fifth graders think of the library media center as a separate subject, such as art, music, or physical education, it is difficult for them to fully understand the function of a library. They may come to think that the library media center has a subject matter of its own on which they will be instructed and graded. This misconception deters them from developing long-standing good habits of library and information use. An understanding of the interrelatedness of subjects and the role of the library as a storehouse for information is brought about by the close connection of the location and interpretation skills learned in the library media center along with the questions raised and topics covered in subject area instruction.

Many of the activities in this section are to be used in conjunction with an assignment in a subject area of the curriculum. This coordination is highly beneficial to subject area instruction as well as to library skills instruction. The library media center can accommodate the children's widening range of abilities, maturity levels, and personal interests in a way that is not possible in even the most carefully planned text-oriented instruction.

You may not want or be able to coordinate the library media center program with instruction in every subject area. Choose one or two subjects in the curriculum in which the topics covered, as well as the inclination of the teacher, lend themselves to cooperative instruction and planning.

To initiate coordinated instruction, meet with the teacher to share objectives. Explain clearly and simply what fifth graders will be learning in the library media center. Determine the topics that the teacher will be covering and the mutual goals you share. These goals will usually be in the area of research and reporting techniques. Clearly establish what skills each of you will introduce, instruct, and reinforce. Continue to have casual conversations and an occasional planning session as the year progresses. Keep the planning sessions short, to the point, and productive for both parties. Frequent drawn-out planning sessions tend to discourage even the most enthusiastic teacher.

Dewey Decimal System

In the fifth grade, the children have learned to use decimals in mathematics. This is an appropriate time to teach the function of the decimal point in the Dewey Decimal System. To locate materials on the shelves, the children need to understand that 596.15 comes before 596.2. They can also understand that the decimal point is used to create a wider range of subdivisions within each of the ten Dewey categories. The activity "Decimal Search," on page 129, provides instruction and practice in using the decimal point.

The children can be led to understand that there are many ways of organizing information. The Dewey Decimal System is the most generally accepted way to organize small library collections. If they think of the Dewey

Decimal System as a model of the ways to classify information and materials so that information and certain materials can be retrieved, they will be able to adapt to other systems. The library media center can become a laboratory for testing one way of organizing and locating materials. The children can be encouraged to think of other classification systems that they know, such as the organization of a supermarket, a department store, a newspaper, or a magazine. They can invent their own classification systems to organize their collections of stamps, rocks, dolls, books, and other things.

This procedure, used to explain classification systems, is referred to as the *information science approach to classification*. It prepares children to be information seekers and users during their adult lives. Understanding the information science approach is one of the underlying goals of the library media center program.

The children should not be required to memorize the Dewey Decimal System. Instead, they should be given a clear understanding of how the system works. They should understand that the two general categories of materials are fiction and nonfiction. Nonfiction is divided into 10 categories, which may be subdivided into 10 more categories, which may be subdivided into increasingly more precise subtopics. You might have them consider how the categories of biography and fiction can be accommodated within the 10 categories. This kind of question increases the children's understanding of the system. When they consider that biographies can be included in the 900's and that fiction can be classified with literature in the 800's, they reveal a deep understanding of this way of organizing materials.

No amount of discussing and thinking about the classification system is sufficient in itself to learn to use the library media center. Nothing can take the place of actually following the steps to locate some specific piece of information that is needed.

Research and Reporting Techniques

Fifth graders use the materials in the library media center to research and to report on topics in subject areas of the curriculum. They need to have a clear understanding of how to proceed. Besides the ability to locate information on a topic, they need the ability to combine the information from several sources into a presentable report. This is not an easy task.

Children have a tendency to begin taking notes as soon as they open a book. They often copy word for word without understanding the meaning of what they are writing. It is important for them to understand the difference between an overview of a topic and the details of a topic. The activity "Combining Information," on page 139, provides the opportunity for students to work through the steps of gathering information for a report. In this activity the children first get an overview of their topic without taking any notes. From the overview, they select several important subtopics. Then notes are taken on the details of each subtopic. In this way the children experience the value of getting an overview of a topic before becoming overly involved with details.

The example used is that of a visitor walking on a street in a strange city. The visitor becomes absorbed in the many detailed sights and sounds in the small area surrounding him and does not get a view of what life is like in the city as a whole. That same visitor would have a truer concept of the unfamiliar city were he to go to the top of a tall building and look out at the panoramic view as well as walking along the streets. The details of the small neighborhood would then be in proper perspective with the many other aspects of life in the city. The details fill out the overview and give it meaning.

Once information has been gathered and notes have been taken, the children often have difficulty compiling the information into a meaningful report. The activity presented here helps a student to organize his or her notes. The children are asked to read through their subtopics and number them in the order that they want to report on them. Next, the children write a paragraph on each subtopic using the details that they have gathered. After that, they write an introductory paragraph and a closing paragraph. In this way, the children work through the entire research and reporting process step by step.

Methods used in researching and reporting vary greatly from one individual to another. The children should be encouraged to adapt the procedure suggested here to their individual style and to develop their own ways of gathering information and reporting. This procedure gives them a starting place by offering some practical suggestions on the techniques to use. It is not meant to be considered as the right way or the only method. It does provide all of the children with an opportunity to experience success in researching and reporting and to gain confidence in their own developing abilities.

Bibliography

The ability to list the sources used in gathering information is extended in the fifth grade to include more detailed information that is more precisely cited. The student learns to cite the publisher and the copyright date of a book in addition to the title and author. The student learns to cite audiovisual materials and periodicals. Rules for underlining and standard punctuation are learned. Have the students put these skills into practice whenever possible by requiring them to cite the sources for research and reporting.

Reference Sources

In the fifth grade, the children learn about the variety of sources in the reference collection. They become aware that the reference collection has sources on people, places, and things. They begin to determine which reference books have information about one or the other of these categories and either to select the appropriate source to answer a specific question or to gather a certain type of information.

A number of activities in this section provide opportunities for children to use biographical dictionaries, atlases, and almanacs. They become familiar with these sources and begin to use the specific kind of information that they contain. Fifth grade children will need to be reminded and encouraged to use these sources on their own. Recommend a variety of sources rather than directing them immediately to an encyclopedia for every reference question.

Audiovisual Materials

Fifth grade children often enjoy supplementing their research with audiovisual materials, such as filmstrips, filmloops, records, and cassettes. Viewing and listening equipment is simple to operate and may be used by one child or a small group of children.

The children can become aware that audiovisual materials do not replace the detailed, in-depth information in books. Audiovisual materials offer a visual concept of a topic that can seldom be offered by print materials. A visual presentation often clarifies a student's understanding and provides an image, which can be referred to in further reading and learning. Students need to understand the difference in the function of print and nonprint materials to determine when to use each in learning.

Producing Audiovisual Materials

Literacy is the ability to read and write. Visual literacy is the ability to interpret what is seen and to express ideas visually. Throughout the grade levels of the library media center program, the children have expressed their ideas through drawing. In the fifth grade, they are given opportunities to use visuals in reporting.

The activity "Making Slides," on page 137, instructs students in photographing illustrations to make slides, which supplement their oral reports. In this way the children present the information that they have gathered and report it to others using visual as well as verbal skills.

There are many other uncomplicated types of visuals that the children can make. Transparencies may be drawn with greased pencils. Old filmstrips, which have been soaked in bleach, may be reused by drawing on them with colored pencils. The opaque projector may be used to enlarge illustrations. Manual films may be made by drawing a sequence and using an overhead or opaque projector to show it. There are many additional simple production techniques that you can teach children.

Children working together in small groups can most satisfactorily produce audiovisual materials. The confusion and commotion of large groups often interferes with accomplishing the task. On the other hand, individual children can become overwhelmed and discouraged with the many steps involved in planning and showing a finished product.

Opportunities to develop production techniques and the experience of producing visuals to express ideas are important in developing visual literacy abilities. Being able to produce visuals gives children opportunities to experience visual media from the inside. In this way, they become more able to fully understand visual messages. The children use television to supply much of their information and entertainment outside of school. Developing skills to understand and to interpret what they see and hear has become an important part of the library media center instructional program.

Interpreting Television Messages

In the fifth grade, children distinguish between fiction and nonfiction television and have opportunities to develop techniques to find meaning in both types of programs. Through discussion, they become aware of the differences in the kind of attention they give to each type of program. In fictional television programs, the emphasis is on the experience and on the emotions felt at the time the program is viewed. In nonfictional television programs, the information obtained from the program is significant.

After they have viewed a nonfiction program, they draw the main point and details from the presentation. The activity "How Birds Adapt," on page 142, develops the abilities to do this. After they have viewed a fictional television program, they analyze the feelings of the characters and relate them to their own experiences. In both cases, they use their abilities of recalling, summarizing, paraphrasing, and extending to understand what they view.

Periodicals

The fifth grader analyzes the content of magazines in preparation for using periodicals as a research source. In the activity "Magazine Reports," on page 136, the children determine the scope and audience of the magazines in the library media center collection. They learn that magazines are a source of current information in various areas of special interest. Encourage fifth grade children to sample a variety of magazines and to follow those magazines that appeal to their personal interests.

Literature Appreciation

The children become more familiar with the various types of fiction and other literature in the collection. They begin to recognize the distinguishing characteristics of different kinds of literature. Many have developed preferences for certain kinds. These preferences are often quite short-lived, however. A child who reads nothing but mysteries might suddenly ask to be directed to the poetry section. Many different things can spark an interest in a certain type of literature. It might be a television program, a suggestion from a friend, or a lesson in language arts.

Book Talks

Book talks are an excellent means for you to introduce new books to fifth grade children. You can talk about books on one theme or by one author. Occasionally give a potpourri book talk, which includes a short description of different kinds of books that appeal to a wide range of personal interests and abilities. A potpourri book talk is one of the activities in this section (see page 138).

Writing to Understand a Type of Literature

The technique of writing a specific kind of literature to more fully understand it was introduced in fourth grade, using mystery and fantasy. In the fifth grade, it is extended to include science fiction and biography.

Science Fiction

The activity "Science Fiction," on page 128, has the children write science fiction stories. Students learn to analyze science fiction to determine what is the scientific information upon which the story is based. The children combine scientific facts, which they have learned through characters, a setting, and a plot, to write a science fiction story. In this way, they understand the distinction between fiction and nonfiction and are better able to evaluate and to select this type of literature. They come to appreciate the knowledge and the skill of science fiction writers. Writing science fiction stories is a creative and challenging activity for them. They greatly enjoy sharing their own stories with one another.

Biography

Ten-year-olds are aware of individual interests and the variety of ways people live their lives. Biography is especially interesting to many children at this age. The activities in this section help children to understand the ways information is gathered for biographies and autobiographies. By writing biographical sketches and memoirs, the children learn how this literature is researched and compiled. In this way, they can appreciate and evaluate this kind of literature.

Using writing skills to more fully appreciate and understand what is read is effective in fifth grade. Most children derive satisfaction from writing. Some will need help to get started. Have those who experience difficulty talk about their ideas or lack of ideas with you or another child. This usually gets them over that initial incapability. Sometimes it helps to tell a child who has trouble getting started to write the middle and come back to the beginning later. Once started, the ideas usually come rapidly. Don't let them become too bothered by spelling and punctuation. Suggest that they write as though they were speaking to another person. Encourage them to write down their ideas and to attend to other details afterward. Recommend that the children reread their writing to make corrections and additions.

When the children share their stories, create an accepting, appreciative atmosphere. The children will recognize an exceptionally well-written story, but don't embarrass those who have not achieved excellence. Remember that the purpose is to provide all of the children with the opportunity to be authors.

Learning in Groups

Ten-year-olds enjoy the company of children their own age. They seek the approval of other children and need a sense of belonging. They are inclined to be somewhat critical of themselves, as well as others, and often show prejudice. At this age, children are more able to work with others. Leadership abilities, as well as the ability to follow the leadership of others, begin to develop.

Fifth grade children are suited to group activities. Although they should have opportunities to develop their individual abilities to locate and to use library media center materials, they should also be given opportunities to work in small groups.

Research and reporting are areas in which group work can be especially productive. The children are beginning to develop skills to gather pieces of information and to combine them into a presentable form. Small group projects to collect and to combine data can increase individual abilities at this stage. Each child can participate, some emerging as leaders, others as followers. By combining their efforts, no individual need be overwhelmed by the extent of the project. At times you may need to moderate and smooth a situation by offering your assistance to enable the children to proceed to a satisfying conclusion.

Games

Ten-year-olds are motivated by competition. Group games are a useful means of instruction and review at this age. Several games have been included as activities in this section. These games can be fun for all of the fifth graders if the rules are clearly understood and the game is fairly played.

Summary

In the fifth grade, children use the library media center collection to do research and reports in subject areas and for entertainment. They analyze the Dewey Decimal System as a prototype, or model, of a way to organize information so it can be retrieved. Fifth graders learn techniques to gather and to combine information in a presentable form. They increase their abilities to evaluate materials and to make satisfying selections.

FIFTH GRADE LIBRARY SKILLS
CHECKLIST AND ACTIVITIES

The following presents a sequential checklist of library and information skills to be developed at the fifth grade level and suggested activities for teaching specific skills. Each activity is keyed to a major skill objective at this level and is ready for your immediate use or adaptation.

Class _____

I. Location Skills
A. Card Catalog
1. Understands that the card catalog is an index to the library media center collection
2. Can locate materials using call numbers on catalog cards
3. Can use the card catalog to locate materials by author, title, and subject

    a. **Alphabetizing**
      (1) Can alphabetize by interior letters of words
      (2) Can interpret drawer labels on the card catalog

    b. **Subject Headings**
      (1) Understands and uses cross-references
      (2) Can convert own terminology into that used in subject headings
      (3) Can be specific when looking up subject

    c. **Descriptive Information**
      (1) Can interpret information on catalog cards, e.g., type and level of material, publication date, whether illustrated
      (2) Can use information on catalog cards to compile a simple bibliography

B. Fiction and Nonfiction
1. Understands the difference between fiction and nonfiction
2. Knows various kinds of fiction: adventure, science, realistic, mystery, historical, fantasy, sports, humorous
3. Has read some of each of the various types of fiction
4. Can use the nonfiction collection as a source of information

C. Dewey Decimal System
1. Understands that the purpose of the system is to pull together materials on the same subject and literary form
2. Understands the ten main classes
3. Understands that the ten main classes can be divided and subdivided into more specific subjects
4. Can locate materials using call numbers

D. Reference Collection
1. Can distinguish the unique characteristics of various reference sources
2. Can determine the reference source most appropriate for a specific purpose

    a. **Encyclopedias**
      (1) Can use cross-references to locate information in an encyclopedia
      (2) Can use indexes to locate information in an encyclopedia

    b. **Dictionaries**
      (1) Can use alphabetical order and guide words in dictionary work
      (2) Can obtain definitions from dictionary entries
      (3) Can use pronunciation key
      (4) Can use specialized English language dictionaries

    c. **Other Reference Tools**
      (1) Can use almanacs to find statistics and other facts
      (2) Can use atlases to locate places

Class _____

E. Biographical Sources
1. Can locate information about a person
2. Knows the different types of biographical materials and can locate information in each
3. Can locate information about a person in the collective biography collection

F. Periodicals
1. Is familiar with periodicals of varying scope and purpose
2. Knows periodicals are a source of current information

G. Indexes
1. Knows indexes provide access to information by subject in book and reference sources
2. Can locate information on a subject using a book's index
3. Can locate information in an encyclopedia using an index
4. Can use cross-references to locate information in an index
5. Is aware of indexes to information beyond the library media center collection

H. Vertical Files
1. Knows the type of material found in vertical files, e.g., pictures, clippings, pamphlets
2. Can locate vertical file materials for an appropriate purpose

I. Audiovisual Materials and Equipment
1. Knows that information comes in a variety of formats
2. Can locate materials in the audiovisual collection
3. Can operate equipment in order to use materials
4. Can produce own audiovisual materials when appropriate, e.g., to illustrate a report

II. Interpretation Skills
A. Evaluation and Selection Techniques
1. Understands the various forms of literature
2. Is acquainted with authors and their works
3. Can select materials for leisure reading
4. Can use the various parts of a book to determine scope, format, timeliness, and to locate and document information

B. Research and Reporting Techniques
1. Can locate materials to discover what others have learned about a topic
2. Can use ideas gained through different materials
3. Can carry research through to a conclusion
4. Can present information in a written report and/or an oral presentation
5. Can make a bibliography of author, title, publisher, and date for research assignments

C. Listening and Viewing Skills
1. Attends to the sights and sounds of the instructional situation
2. Interprets what is heard and seen
3. Can recall, summarize, and paraphrase what is listened to and viewed

D. Literature Appreciation
1. Is familiar with various forms of literature
2. Can interpret meaning from many forms of literature

© 1981 by The Center for Applied Research in Education, Inc.

I. LOCATION SKILLS   A. Card Catalog

CROSS-REFERENCES

An extension of an activity used in the fourth grade, this exercise provides an opportunity for the children to use cross-references to find appropriate subject headings. The children now work individually and with more difficult terms. This is a difficult concept, and practice should be provided to reinforce learning:

Time: 30 to 45 minutes
Materials: Pencils
       Paper
       Chalkboard or chart
Preparation: Choose 10 cross-references from the card catalog. List them on the chalkboard, omitting the "See" or "See also" reference. (See example at end of activity directions.)
Activity Directions:
Have the children copy the cross-references from the chalkboard. Explain that if they were looking for material on these topics, they would need to use cross-references to find the subject heading used in the card catalog. Have the children look up the topics in the card catalog, find the subject headings by using the cross-reference, and use the subject heading to find the call number. Ask the children to write the subject heading for each cross-reference and the corresponding call number.

Allow 20 minutes to complete the task. Offer assistance to students as they need it. Have children who experience difficulty work with partners.

When the children have completed the assignment, have them share what they found. Write the subject heading on the board next to the corresponding cross-reference and call number as each is named by the students.

Examples of cross-references to use in this activity include the following:

Body see *Anatomy*

Indians, Navaho see *Navaho Indians*

Hostesses, Airlines see *Airlines—Flight Attendant*

Teenage see *Adolescence*

Doctor see *Physicians*

Folklore see also *Fairy Tales*

Freedom of Press see also *Censorship*

Freedom of Speech see also *Free Speech*

Pioneer see *Frontier and Pioneer Life*

Variations: The children may be required to locate a book for each subject after the call number has been determined.

I. LOCATION SKILLS   B. Fiction and Nonfiction

SCIENCE FICTION

This activity helps students understand the difference between fiction and nonfiction and identify the various types of fiction and forms of literature.

NOTE: *The activity is most effective when coordinated with the language arts and science curricula.*

Time: Five 30-minute sessions

Materials: Science Fiction collection of the library media center
Filmstrip: *A Wrinkle in Time* by Madeline L'Engle.
New York: Milton Brody, Inc., 1972.

Filmstrip projector
Record player
Paper
Pencils

Activity Directions:

Session I—Direct the students to develop a definition for science fiction by brainstorming. As they share their ideas, write them on the chalkboard. Have one of the students read the definition from a dictionary.

Discuss how to locate science fiction in a library: "Science fiction is intermingled with the fiction collection. How do you find a science fiction book?" Have two students look up the subject heading *Science Fiction* in the card catalog and read the call numbers for the class to write down. Then have the children locate science fiction books to read.

Sessions II and III—Show parts 1 and 2 of the filmstrip. Have the students look for evidences of science fiction in the story to be discussed after the filmstrip, that is, the use of scientific terms and concepts in addition to the development of characters and plot.

During the discussion following the filmstrip, have the students identify science-fiction elements by giving specific examples. At the conclusion of the discussion, ask the students to think about and to plan a science fiction story that they would like to write.

Session IV—Have the students write a science fiction story of their own. Remind them to include scientific principles and terms as well as characters and a plot.

Session V—Call on students to read their stories, drawing the class's attention to the elements of a science fiction story. Some children who are shy about reading their own story may be willing to have a classmate read it for them.

Variations: This technique may be adapted to other forms of literature. Reading a sample of the literary form may be used in place of showing a filmstrip. Films or videotapes may also be used.

I. LOCATION SKILLS   C. Dewey Decimal System

DIFFERENT WAYS TO ORGANIZE

This activity deepens the understanding that the purpose of the classification system is to pull together materials on the same subject and literary form.

Time: 30 minutes

Materials: Chalkboard or chart

Library media center collection

Activity Directions:

Through a discussion, lead the children to define a classification system. Have them think of classification systems that they know, other than the one used in the library media center. For example, they can examine the ones used to organize a grocery store or a department store or the ones used to organize a newspaper or magazine.

On the chalkboard, write the following numbers in columns, leaving a space after each one so that the children can fill in the subject of each category: 001, 100, 200, 300, 400, 500, 600, 700, 800, 900.

Divide the class into groups of two or three, assign a number to each group, and have them go to the shelves to investigate and to determine the main subject or subjects included within that numerical category. Have each group write the subject next to the number on the chalkboard. After each group has completed the investigation and has added its subject to the list, review all of the numbers and corresponding subjects with the class.

Follow-up: Following this activity, introduce the concept that there are other ways to organize materials and information. The Dewey Decimal System is the generally accepted classification system used in small libraries. New and more efficient systems may be devised at some time. Have the children suggest some other ways that library media center materials might be organized.

I. LOCATION SKILLS   C. Dewey Decimal System

DECIMAL SEARCH

This activity provides an understanding that the 10 main classes can be divided and subdivided into more specific subjects. In the fifth grade, the children usually learn decimals in mathematics and are ready to understand the function of the decimal point in the Dewey Decimal System.

Time: 30 minutes

Materials: Chalkboard or chart

Library media center collection

Activity Directions:

Demonstrate and describe the purpose of the decimal point by using the following example. (Put the example on the chalkboard or a chart.)

796   Athletic and outdoor sports
796.3   Ball games
796.31   Ball thrown or hit by hand
796.33   Ball driven by foot
796.34   Racquet games
796.35   Ball driven by a club, mallet, or bat
796.352   Golf
796.357   Baseball

Divide the class into groups of two or three children. Assign each group one of the above Dewey numbers. Have the children locate a book with the corresponding call number. Alternate turns so that all of the children do not crowd into the section at one time.

Have each group report to the class in the order that the books are found on the shelves. Have the children show the book and name the title, author, and call number. After each group has returned and has had a turn, have the children return the books to the proper places in the collection.

Follow-up: This activity may be repeated, using a variety of other Dewey Decimal sequences.

I. LOCATION SKILLS   C. Dewey Decimal System

DEWEY DECIMAL GAME

This game provides practice in thinking of subjects within the main categories of the Dewey Decimal System. This practice helps children to better understand how information is organized and to think of terms to use for subject headings.

Time: Two 30-minute sessions

Materials: A chart of the 10 main classes of the Dewey Decimal System.

Preparation: Display a chart of the 10 main classes of the Dewey Decimal System. Commercial charts are available, or you may make one. The chart should show the 10 Dewey categories and their corresponding numbers.

Activity Directions:

Have the class form teams of three or four. Choose one child to be the scorekeeper. Carefully explain the rules of the game. Each team chooses one of the 10 Dewey categories. Every team member will have a turn to name a subject within that category. The teams compete to see which one can name the most subjects within their chosen category.

Have the members of each team sit in a circle facing each other. Have one team start by having a child name the chosen category and a subject within that category. The next child repeats what the former child said and adds a subject of his or her own. The third child repeats all previously named subjects and adds a subject. Continue in this way until a team member forgets the sequence or can't name a new subject.

The teams are awarded a point for each new subject named. The other teams may challenge by raising their hands and stating the error. They also assist the scorekeeper by keeping count of the subjects named.

After each team has had a turn to compete, the team with the highest score wins. Expect to play the game for two sessions because most of the first session is used to learn the game.

Follow-up: This game may be repeated throughout the year.

Variations: A more simple version of this game is to have the children name only the last subject added, rather than naming all of the accumulated subjects.

I. LOCATION SKILLS   D. Reference Collection

USING AN ALMANAC

This activity introduces the almanac as part of the reference collection. It helps children to understand and use the almanac as a source of statistics and current facts.

Time: 30 to 40 minutes

Materials: One almanac for each child in the class

> *The World Almanac.*
> Newspaper Enterprise Association
> 1278 West Ninth Street
> Cleveland, Ohio 44113
>
> Paper
> Pencils

NOTE: *With most reference materials, children can learn in small groups by sharing a book. The small print and compact nature of almanacs, however, makes use by more than one person at a time difficult. It is easier to learn to use the almanac if each student has a copy. Paperback copies are relatively inexpensive and may be used for instruction for several years. A set of almanacs may be shared by the library media specialists in a school district.*

Activity Directions:

Explain that almanacs are a source of current facts and statistics issued annually. Give each child an almanac and ask them to scan to find the various topics covered. List the topics on the chalkboard as the children name them. Read through the list to review the scope of information covered.

Have the children look for the different kinds of ways in which the information is presented, such as maps, charts, graphs. As these are named, write them on the chalkboard.

Have the children locate the index and raise their hands to indicate that they have found it. Ask what is different about this index from most other indexes that they have used. Establish the fact that this index is in the front of the book and that the main access to the information in an almanac is through the index.

Have the children use the index to find one fact about each topic listed on the chalkboard. Allow 15 minutes to complete the task.

Name each topic and have the children name the fact that they found about the topic. Have them describe the way the fact was presented. Choose several children to describe the procedure they followed to locate information on the topics.

Follow-up: Encourage the children to use almanacs individually to answer questions on current facts or statistics.

I. LOCATION SKILLS   D. Reference Collection

USING AN ATLAS

This activity acquaints students with atlases as a source in the reference collection and provides practice in locating places in an atlas. This activity is not intended to provide in-depth instruction in map skills. Map skills are usually a part of the social studies curriculum. This lesson should be coordinated with social studies map skills instruction. The children should have an understanding of basic map skills before participating in this activity.

Time: 30 minutes

Materials: The atlases from the library media center reference collection, for example:

New Cosmopolitan World Atlas. Rand McNally and Co.

Hammond World Atlas. Hammond Inc.

The World Book Atlas. Field Enterprises Educational Corp.

World Atlas. Rand McNally and Co.

Paper
Pencils

Activity Directions:

Discuss the definition of an atlas and ask when it should be used. Show the students the different atlases in the collection and read the title of each.

Divide the class into five small groups and give an atlas to each one. Allow the children to look through the atlas for a few minutes. Ask them to describe how they would find a particular place in the atlas. Have each group turn to the index. Call attention to the alphabetical order of the index.

Tell the children to look up the town in which they live. Have each group describe the information given in the index citation.

Have the children turn to the page given in the citation. Discuss the longitude and latitude key. Have the children in each group take turns to locate the place on the map. Provide an opportunity for each group to describe how they located the place in the atlas that they used. Compare the similarities and differences of the organization of the atlases.

Follow-up: Encourage the students to use the atlases individually in order to locate and to gather other information on places.

I. LOCATION SKILLS   E. Biographical Sources

SOURCES OF BIOGRAPHY

This activity provides an opportunity to review four sources of biography in the library media center collection. This helps children to understand the type of information contained in each of the following sources: biography, collective biography, autobiography, reference biography.

Time: 30 minutes
Materials: Paper
                Pencils
Activity Directions: Write four types of biography on the chalkboard and briefly review the definition of each.

	answer code
Biography	B
Autobiography	A
Collective Biography	C
Biographical Dictionary	R

NOTE: *Although biographical dictionaries are a form of collective biography, they are located in the reference collection and are used as a source of quick reference. You might prefer to use the term reference biography, instead of biographical dictionary.*

Have the children number their papers from one to ten. Ask them to choose the best source of information for each of the following. Ask them what biographical source they would use if they were asked to do these things:

answer code

1. Compare the careers of several baseball players.   C
2. Describe the early life of Abraham Lincoln.   B
3. Discuss what Helen Keller considered important in her
   own life.   A
4. Compare the accomplishments of several presidents.   C
5. Discover why Clara Barton is famous.   R
6. Gather some stories about Muhammad Ali.   B
7. Describe the lives of some black leaders.   C
8. Discover who Aaron Copland was.   R
9. Read some of Ben Franklin's diary.   A
10. Find out whether there are two famous people named
    J. P. Morgan.   R

Have the children exchange papers while they go over the 10 biographical information situations. Call on various children to give the source for each activity and the reason for their choice.

Follow-up: Using other biographical information situations, repeat this lesson if you feel that the children do not fully understand the difference between the biographical sources.

I. LOCATION SKILLS   E. Biographical Sources

COMPARING BIOGRAPHIES

This activity allows students to practice locating information about a person. It requires the children to find both collective and individual biographies and to compare the information in each. Attention is drawn to collective biographies, which are a source that students easily overlook. In this activity, the children work with a partner to encourage combining information and discussing findings to further increase understanding.

Time: Two 30-minute sessions or one 45-minute to one-hour session
Materials: Paper
             Pencils
Preparation: Write the name of a famous person at the top of each piece of paper. Make a paper for half of the children in the class. Be certain that information about each person may be found in both the biography and in the collective biography collection. The following list names people that you might use.

Abraham Lincoln

George Washington

John Kennedy

Louis Pasteur

Marie Curie

Thomas Edison

Albert Einstein

Mary McLeod Bethune

Paul Robeson

Gale Sayers

Peter Tchaikovsky

Christopher Columbus

Activity Directions:

Session I—Have the children work in partners. Distribute the papers marked with the names of famous persons. Explain that they are going to find information about the person in an individual biography and a collective biography. Direct them to find first an individual biography. Discuss how a person can locate a biography. Review the fact that the call number contains the subject's name instead of the author's name. Explain that biographies may be found by going directly to the shelf and looking under the subject's name.

Use the individual biography to find out why the person is famous. Have the children describe how they will use this information to find a collective biography. Discuss the use of subject headings in the card catalog to locate a collective biography. Describe what is listed under the call number 920. While the students are locating the biographies, assist those who are experiencing difficulty.

When the students have found both sources, have them write the title and call number of each source on their papers. Have them look through both sources and discuss with their partners the difference between the information in each. Tell them to use the paper to make notes on examples of differences.

Session II—Give the students 10 minutes to relocate their biographies and prepare to report to the class. Provide an opportunity for each group to report their findings to the class. Have them say who their famous person was and why he or she is famous. Have them explain how they located each biography and describe the differences that they found between the two sources.

Lead the students to conclude that an individual biography is usually about a person's whole life, whereas a collective biography usually gives limited information about why the person was famous.

Follow-up: Encourage the children to use the collective biography collection.

I. LOCATION SKILLS   F. Periodicals

MAGAZINE REPORTS

This activity provides an opportunity for children to become familiar with periodicals from the library media center collection that vary in scope and purpose.

Time: Two 30-minute sessions

Materials: Periodicals from the library media center collection

Activity Directions:

Session I—In a discussion, clearly define what a periodical is. Establish the following concepts. Periodicals are magazines and newspapers that are published periodically, that is, daily, weekly, monthly, or quarterly. Periodicals are a source of recent information. They are usually in soft cover and are disposable.

Have one child read the titles of the magazines in the library media center collection. List the titles on the chalkboard as they are read. Have each child choose a magazine to read and report on to the class. Ask the children to come to the following session prepared to answer three questions about the magazine:

1. How often do the issues appear?
2. What is its scope, or what information does it contain?
3. What is its audience, or who would probably read it?

Session II—Have each child describe the magazine that he or she reviewed. Write the three questions to be answered by each child on the chalkboard. The children may give added information about the magazine, but they must include the required information.

Follow-up: The children may be given time to read magazines in the library media center. You may also want to circulate magazines.

I. LOCATION SKILLS   G. Indexes

SPECIFIC INFORMATION

This activity provides practice in interpreting citations in indexes. It helps children to select the specific information that they need from an index.

Time: 30 to 40 minutes

Materials: Paper

Pencils

Nonfiction books with indexes

Preparation: This activity should be done while children are researching and reporting on a subject area of the curriculum. After the children have chosen topics that require specific information, use this activity to help them to locate this type of information.

Activity Directions:

Review the use of indexes to find information that is not listed in the table of contents of a book or alphabetically in an encyclopedia. Explain that under the general topic in an index are citations of more specific information on the topic. Tell the children to find one source on their topics that includes an index. Allow 10 minutes for them to find the books and to scan the index. Assist children experiencing difficulty.

Write "425-428" and "67" on the chalkboard. Have the children explain which citation indicates the most information and why.

Have each child use the index in the book to locate information that applies specifically to his or her topic and make a note of the pages cited. Give each student an opportunity to describe the citations in the index that he or she will use to locate specific information.

Follow-up: Have the students continue their research by using the citations to locate the specific information and by reporting on their topics in the subject area.

I. LOCATION SKILLS   I. Audiovisual Materials and Equipment

MAKING SLIDES

In this small group activity, the children makes slides to illustrate reports. They come to understand that information is presented in a variety of formats and they have an opportunity to report in a visual form.

Time: One 30- to 40-minute session with the entire class and subsequent 30- to 40-minute sessions with groups of three or four children

Materials: Ektagraphic Kit, consisting of camera, stand, flash cubes, and film

Black construction paper

Preparation: This activity should be coordinated with a research and oral reporting assignment in a subject area.

Activity Directions:

Explain to the children that they may make slides to accompany an oral presentation that they are preparing for a subject area. Demonstrate how to use the Ektagraphic kit to make slides. Use a piece of black construction paper to frame an illustration in a book so it can be photographed. Several children should have turns taking pictures of different illustrations while the other children watch.

Have the children locate three illustrations on the topic of their oral presentation. Explain that clear, uncomplicated illustrations of moderate size will offer the best results. Tell the children to make a note of where they found the illustration. Assist children in finding appropriate illustrations.

Arrange to have the children return to the library media center in small groups to photograph the illustrations that they chose.

Follow-up: Develop the film and give the slides to the children to use with their oral report. Instruct the children on how to operate the slide projector for their presentations.

II. INTERPRETATION SKILLS   A. Evaluation and Selection Techniques

BOOK TALK ACTIVITY

The following book talk activity acquaints children with a variety of books in the library media center and encourages them to select some of the books to read.

Time: 30 to 40 minutes

Materials: Books from the library media center collection

Preparation: Prepare a display of 10 to 20 high-interest books. Include books that would appeal to a variety of tastes and a wide range of reading ability. Select both fiction and nonfiction titles.

Activity Directions:

Briefly describe each book. Say whether it is fiction or nonfiction. Comment on the characters and plot or on the information in the book. Tell just enough about it to arouse curiosity and stimulate interest. Describe 10 to 20 books in this way, allowing approximately one minute per book.

As you tell about the books, have the children note the call numbers of the books that sound especially appealing to them. Encourage the children to choose one of the books on display to read. Assist students who have difficulty finding a book that interests them. Remind the children to keep the list of call numbers of the books that interested them so they can refer to it in the future, when looking for books to read.

After the children have selected the books, provide 5 to 10 minutes for quiet reading. At this time, the children will begin the book; such beginning encourages them to continue reading on their own.

Follow-up: After the children have read the books, provide an opportunity for them to express what they thought about the book and whether they agreed with your assessment.

This book talk and reading activity may be followed by the next activity in which the children make advertising posters of books that they have recently read.

II. INTERPRETATION SKILLS   A. Evaluation and Selection Techniques

BOOK POSTERS

This activity enables children to share their knowledge of authors and their works and to learn from each other. It provides opportunities for children to share materials that they have enjoyed.

Time: Two 30-minute sessions
Materials: Construction paper of assorted colors
                   Crayons
                   Pencils
                   Colored pencils
                   Marking pens
                   Paste
                   Scissors

Activity Directions:

Have the children choose a book that they have recently read and would recommend to other children. They may choose a fiction or nonfiction book that is in the library media center collection.

Explain that they are going to make a poster, which will be posted in the library media center, to advertise the book. Each advertisement should include the title, author, and call number of the book. Encourage the children to write a brief description of the book that would make someone want to read it. Have them illustrate their posters attractively to catch the attention of the children coming to the library media center. Show examples of book advertisements in the *School Library Journal* or the *Booklist* and other sources.

When all of the children have finished their posters, have each child show his or her poster and tell the others about it.

Follow-up: In the library media center, display the posters advertising favorite books.

II. INTERPRETATION SKILLS   B. Research and Reporting Techniques

COMBINING INFORMATION

This activity provides practice in combining information from different sources to present in a report. It helps children to more fully understand the functions of notetaking and outlining.

Time: Three 30-minute sessions
Materials: Books from the nonfiction collection
                   Encyclopedias
                   Paper
                   Pencils

Preparation: This activity should be coordinated with an assignment in a subject area of the curriculum. The activity calls for researching several sources and combining the information gathered into a short written report.

Activity Directions:

Session I—Have the children locate two sources on one topic: one an encyclopedia article, and the other a book from the nonfiction collection. Explain that they are going to take information from the two sources and combine it into a report.

Have the children think about the difference between walking the streets of an unfamiliar city and going to the top of a tall building to get an overview of the same city. Discuss the advantage of getting an overview before becoming too involved with details. Explain that an overview helps to put the details into proper perspective.

Ask the children to quickly read through the encyclopedia article to get an overview of the topic. Explain that they should not become too concerned with details at first. Caution the children against taking notes as soon as they begin. Direct them to give themselves time to get acquainted with the topic first. Allow 15 to 20 minutes for reading through to get an overview.

After the children have finished reading, have them write three to five main areas of interest under the topic. Direct them to leave a space after each subtopic to fill in 5 to 10 details. Encourage the children who have difficulty determining subtopics to discuss what they read about the topic, and assist them in selecting subtopics.

Session II—Explain that now that they have an overview of their topics and have determined some subtopics, they are ready to find details about each subtopic. Have the children use both the encyclopedia article and the nonfiction book to gather details and to list them under each subtopic. Explain that they do not need to write sentences, but should write down the words that express the ideas. Assist the children who need help.

Session III—Explain that they are now ready to write a report using the information they they have gathered. Have them read through their subtopics and number them in the order in which they want to report them.

Have the children write a paragraph about each subtopic using the details from their notes. Remind the children to start each paragraph with a sentence introducing the subtopic.

After they have completed the paragraphs, have them write an introductory paragraph that describes what they are going to write about. Have them write a closing paragraph that draws conclusions or summarizes their report.

Follow-up: Have the children proofread their reports and make a final copy including a bibliography of the sources they used. This activity may be repeated with other topics.

II. INTERPRETATION SKILLS   B. Research and Reporting Techniques

CITING THE SOURCE

This activity reviews bibliographic skills learned in the fourth grade. Writing a bibliography is a difficult skill to master. The children will need to review, practice, and have opportunities to correct errors. This lesson expands bibliographic citations learned in the fourth grade, including author, title, publisher, and copyright date. The habit of referring to a sample bibliography is encouraged. This activity should be planned in conjunction with researching and reporting on a subject area of the curriculum.

Time: 30 minutes
Materials: Duplicated copies of sample bibliographies for each child
Paper
Pencils
Preparation: Write and duplicate a sample bibliography, including a citation for a book, encyclopedia, magazine, and filmstrip. (See sample below.)

Activity Directions: Review the definition of a bibliography. Establish the understanding that a bibliography is a list of materials that have something in common. Have the children describe times in which they wrote bibliographies of sources that they used in a report.

Discuss plagiarism and the problem of not giving credit to an author for his or her ideas. Have the children recall when they needed to use quotation marks. Establish the understanding that if they want to use the author's exact words they will need to use quotation marks.

Remind the children that in the fourth grade they made bibliographies listing the author and title of their source of information. Explain that in the fifth grade they are going to expand their bibliographies to include other information about the source.

Distribute the sample bibliography. Have the children study the bibliography and name the added features that they notice. List the additions on the chalkboard as they are named by the children, for example:

All titles are underlined.
Publishers and dates are included.
Filmstrips are listed.
Punctuation is included.

Discuss these new features and answer any questions.

Give each child a book from the nonfiction collection. Have them write a bibliographic citation for the book using the sample bibliography as a guide. Collect the papers at the end of the session.

Follow-up: Examine the papers to determine which children need additional individual instruction. Repeat the exercise with a variety of materials: filmstrips, magazines, and encyclopedias.

Arrange with the teacher to correct all bibliographies turned in with reports. Throughout the year, offer individual assistance to children when they are writing bibliographies.

SAMPLE BIBLIOGRAPHY

Book	Andrews, Roy Chapman. <u>All About Dinosaurs</u>, Random House, 1953.
Encyclopedia	"Dinosaur." <u>The World Book Encyclopedia</u>, Vol. 5, pp. 170-173.
Filmstrip	<u>Dinosaurs</u>. National Geographic Society. Filmstrip.
Magazine	"Dinosaurs." <u>Science Digest</u>. September 1977, pp. 31-32.

II. INTERPRETATION SKILLS   C. Listening and Viewing Skills

HOW BIRDS ADAPT

This activity provides opportunities to attend to the sights and sounds of an audiovisual presentation and to interpret what is seen and heard. It enables children to understand what they view and listen to through recalling, summarizing, paraphrasing, and extending.

Time: 40 minutes

Materials: *The Many Worlds of Nature,* "Of Buds, Beaks, and Behavior," produced by Screenscope, Inc.*

Other nonfiction television programs may be substituted.

Preparation: This activity should be coordinated with a unit of study in science.

Activity Directions:

Ask a question prior to showing the program to concentrate the children's attention on a certain aspect of the information contained in the program. While the children view the program, have them consider what happens to birds when their habitat is destroyed.

Show the television program, which is 15 minutes in length. After the program, have the children discuss how birds, unlike many other animals, are able to adapt to changing environments. As the children mention them, list on the chalkboard the way birds adapt. Develop the concept that the structures of the birds' beaks enable them to find food in the most hostile environments.

Follow-up: The science teacher may continue to draw on the more detailed information in the program. Encourage the children to read further about birds and adaptation.

Variation: This activity may be adapted to fictional television programs. Prior to the program, ask a question to concentrate the children's attention on the plot of the story and the feelings of the characters. After the viewing, have them discuss the meaning of the story. Encourage them to relate their own experiences to those portrayed in the story.

---

*Screenscope, Inc., Suite 204, 3600 M. St. NW, Washington, D.C. 20007.

II. INTERPRETATION SKILLS   D. Literature Appreciation

AUTOBIOGRAPHY

This activity enables the students to become familiar with autobiographies as a form of literature. Through writing about memories of their own, they develop an understanding that a collection of memories are compiled to tell the story of one's own life, making an autobiography.

Time: Two 30-minute sessions

Materials: Pencils
                        Lined paper

Activity Directions:

Session I—Have the children recall something that happened to them that stands out in their memory. Explain that it might be something funny, happy, or sad, a time when they were very lonely, or especially touched by someone's kindness. Provide time for the children to reflect and remember. Tell the children to go over their thoughts until they have a memory that they want to write down. Explain that it does not have to be a complete story of everything that occurred before and after, but one that tells enough to give a clear picture of why it stands out as something not to be forgotten.

Allow approximately 20 minutes for writing. Assist students who have difficulty getting started by talking to them about how they spend their time; this usually leads to their recalling a memory worth writing down.

Session II—Have the children share their memories with the class. You may have them read aloud or you may have them pass around their writing to individual friends to be read silently.

Explain that if they continued to write their memories, they would have a collection of memoirs and the beginning of an autobiography.

Follow-up: Read portions of autobiographies, such as the following books:

> *Anne Frank: The Diary of a Young Girl.*
> New York: Doubleday and Co., 1967.
>
> *The Story of My Life* by Helen Keller.
> New York: Doubleday and Co., 1954.

II. INTERPRETATION SKILLS   D. Literature Appreciation

BIOGRAPHY

This activity enables the students to become familiar with biographies as a form of literature. Through writing biographies of their own, students take on the perspective of the author and begin to understand this literary form from the inside.

Time: Four 30-minute sessions

Materials: Paper
                        Pencils

Activity Directions:

Session I—Have the children write a story about a person. Explain that it may be someone that they know personally or it may be someone famous. Their biographical sketches should be interesting, have a main point, and have a beginning, middle, and conclusion. Remind them that a biography is nonfiction and what is described in it must actually have happened.

Explain that they should tell about one or two events in the person's life, not attempt to tell his or her whole life story.

Use the rest of the session for gathering information on the person. Discuss possible ways of gathering information by using biographical sources in the library media center, interviewing, or recalling events that they have witnessed. Recommend that they take notes to refer to when writing the sketches.

Session II—Have the children write a biographical sketch about the person of their choice, using the information gathered during the previous session. Assist students who experience difficulty.

Session III—Write the following description of a biography on the chalkboard or chart: "A biography is made up of true facts and experiences about another person." Have the children exchange their biographical sketches with one another. Have them ask the person who reads their paper if their biography fits the description on the chalkboard.

Give them time to make any changes they wish before sharing the biographical sketches with the class. Give each child an opportunity to read his or her biographical sketch to the other children.

Session IV—Continue the read-around until every child has read his or her biographical sketch.

Follow-up: Read a biography aloud to the children and encourage them to borrow and to read biographies from the library media center collection. Some suggested titles are:

John and Sebastian Cabot by Henry Kurtz.
New York: Franklin Watts, 1973.

Christopher Columbus by Susan Heimann.
New York: Franklin Watts, 1973.

Leif Erikson the Lucky by Malcolm C. Jensen.
New York: Franklin Watts, 1979.

Sacajawea by Olive Burt.
New York: Franklin Watts, 1978.

VII. SIXTH GRADE

Preparing for
Secondary School

In sixth grade, students become more independent in their use of the library media center. Research and reporting techniques are improved through practice and use. All previously learned library and information skills are reviewed, and additional individual instruction is given when needed. The students prepare to make the transition from the confines of the elementary school library media center to more independent use of the broader library media center collection in upper schools.

This chapter provides:

- A description of sixth graders' needs in terms of the library program
- A checklist of library skills to be developed at the sixth level
- Activities for teaching specific skills

THE SIXTH GRADE PROGRAM

Eleven-year-olds are in a period of rapid growth, which occurs between the ages of nine and thirteen. There are marked differences among children of this age. Some eleven-year-olds have not yet entered the rapid growth period and remain in the pause that precedes this time. Others are in the midst of the most awkward stage of this uneven growth period. Still others have nearly completed this growth and are emerging from this stage.

Secondary sex characteristics begin to develop. Restlessness, laziness, and awkwardness are a common result of the rapid, uneven growth. The eleven-year-old is listless at times, but is generally highly active. Play tends to be loud and rough. At this age, students enjoy humor and tend to be silly and giddy.

When planning activities for sixth graders, it is important to consider their characteristic behavior. Eleven-year-olds can be extremely critical, unpredictable, and defiant. They want approval and understanding from adults, but they also want opportunities to be independent, to try things on their own.

Review Skills Through Games

One of the most important objectives of the library media center for sixth graders is to provide a complete review of the skills learned in grades kindergarten through five. Reviewing past learning can be extremely dull and boring for students. Sixth graders often become uncooperative in this type of situation. The use of games is an excellent way to enlist the students' cooperative participation in reviewing. The competition of team games motivates them to participate. As they become involved in the challenge and fun of the game, the subject matter is reviewed without resistance.

The "Location Skills Review Game" and "Category Review," on pages 156 and 157, are competitive team games designed to review library and information skills. Sixth graders enjoy playing these games repeatedly. Vary the review questions each time the game is played to cover skills in using the card catalog, nonfiction and fiction categories, Dewey Decimal System, reference collection, biographical sources, periodicals, and indexes. You may choose to review each of the skills areas separately. In this way, you can check off each skill as it is reviewed.

Further Instruction of Skills

As the review games are played and as the students use the library media center, notice any skills that have not been mastered by most of the students. The students will need further instruction in these skills. You may plan additional instruction by adapting an activity from a prior grade or devising an individual instruction worksheet.

There are formal ways to determine whether the students need additional instruction in certain skills. Questions on library skills are often included in standardized basic skills tests taken by the students. Check the results of these tests for feedback on students who need further instruction on a particular skill. You may want to have the sixth graders take a library skills pretest to determine the skills that have not been adequately learned and need reinforcing. There are standardized tests you can purchase, such as the *Test of Library Skills* by Irene Gullett and Frances Hatfield (Marietta, Georgia: Larlin Corporation, 1975) or you may develop one of your own. This type of test should serve as an individual diagnostic instrument, not as an evaluative measure. A student has successfully learned library and information skills if he or she can locate and interpret library media center materials for information and entertainment. No useful purpose is served by evaluating students further in library use. On the other hand, a pretest may be useful in planning instruction on an individual basis.

The use of tests is an individual choice. Many library media specialists resist using formal testing measures to determine library skills learning. You may prefer to observe students as they review skills and as they use the library media center to determine skills that need further instruction. The checklists kept on skills progress are useful in determining areas needing reinforcement.

Avoid going over skills that most students know for the purpose of teaching a few who haven't yet learned the skill. Those students needing extra help probably won't learn through the large group approach if they haven't learned the skills by this time. Activity cards and other kinds of individual and small group instruction are most effective at this point. A good source is *The "Now" Library: A Stations Approach Media Center Teaching Kit* by Mary Margrabe (Washington, D.C.: Acropolis Books, 1973). Personal interest is the key to success in learning these skills. If a student's compelling personal interest is discovered, he or she is more likely to be motivated to learn skills that lead to information and interpretation of materials.

Relationships with peers are important to eleven-year-olds. They resent any activity that appears to cause them to lose status with the group. Individual instruction to reinforce skills should be handled in a sensitive manner that respects the student's feelings and does not injure his or her position in the group.

Independent Use

By the sixth grade, most students are able to use the library media center independently. They have an understanding of the available resources and know the steps to take to locate materials. They usually come to the library media center for a definite purpose, can find the materials that they need, and follow circulation procedures without assistance.

It is important, however, for sixth grade students to become aware that there are times when the assistance of the library media specialist is necessary. An example of such a time occurs when they have used the subject headings in the card catalog that they consider appropriate, but cannot locate material on a topic. Therefore, they need the library media specialist to tell them the subject heading used in the card catalog that is correct for their topic. Another such time occurs when they are not certain about how to use a new reference source and need instruction.

Students should learn that part of a librarian's role is helping people to use the resources of a library. They should understand not to abuse this service of the librarian by asking for help in tasks that they can do for themselves. On the other hand, they should not leave a library without needed materials because they hesitated to ask a librarian for necessary assistance. If sixth graders know when to ask for help, they will be more successful in retrieving materials in the future.

Research and Reporting Techniques

Sixth graders use the library media center to research topics assigned in subject areas of the curriculum. This is an extremely important part of the sixth grade library media center program. All of the previously learned library and information skills are put into practice when they locate materials, combine information from several sources, and report on the information.

The success of this part of the sixth grade library media center program depends upon the research assignments given to the students by subject area teachers. If a subject area teacher has a clear understanding of the library and the information skills of the students, he or she will be able to assign tasks that will require students to use these skills.

Arrange to meet with teachers to plan research assignments. It is often helpful to give teachers specific examples of research assignments that require students to use and to practice library and information skills. Devise ways to provide a team teaching situation to instruct, advise, and assess the students' research projects. Be specific about what each of you will do.

Many research and reporting techniques are improved and refined in the sixth grade. As students become more proficient at researching, they begin to choose more specific topics. Instead of wanting to know everything and anything about a subject, they begin to narrow their topics and to seek specific information about a particular aspect of a topic. This type of information is more difficult to locate and requires more refined location skills.

The uses of indexes in books is essential for finding specific information and details on a topic. Students need to become more familiar with subheadings in indexes. They need to read these more carefully to choose the appropriate feature of the subject that applies to their research topic. If a student is looking for information on air pollution, references to oil spills will not be useful.

After a student has determined the citation that pertains to the specific information needed, he or she may have difficulty locating the information on the page. When sixth graders turn to a page in a book listed in an index citation, many expect to see a heading or a subheading on the topic. If they do not immediately notice an indication of the topic, they often assume there is no reference to the topic on the page. Students need to understand that an index lists insignificant references to a topic as well as substantial information. It takes some digging to find the needed information. The activity "Interpreting Citations," on page 165, requires students to scan a page to locate the topic indicated in the index citation. After the information has been located on a page, the student determines whether it would be useful for a report.

The ability to gather specific information from several sources and combine it into a cohesive report is a difficult skill. It requires a degree of abstraction of which only mature thinkers are capable. This type of thinking emerges in the final stage of development between the ages of twelve and sixteen. At eleven, students are laying the foundation for the development of this skill. Do not expect every sixth grader to submit reports with a succinctly stated hypothesis, substantial data, and well thought-out conclusions. However, every sixth grader can have the experience of working through the process of researching and reporting to develop the techniques that will be needed as abstraction capabilities emerge.

The research and reporting activity "All the Facts," on page 169, is an extension of the fifth grade activity. The sixth grade activity requires students to use more sources, to cover an increased number of subtopics, and to demonstrate greater independence within a clear, simple framework. The framework provided has students divide their topic into subtopics and gather details on the subtopics. Simple instruction for writing reports from notes is also given. Working within this framework should enable students to gather information successfully from various sources and combine it into a clear presentation.

Sources for Research and Reporting

Encourage sixth grade students to use a variety of sources for research and reporting. They should become more proficient at determining the appropriate source for a specific kind of information. Biographical dictionaries and geographical dictionaries are added to the other reference sources that they have had opportunities to use through library media center activities.

Materials in the audiovisual collection are useful for obtaining a visual image of a topic. Through an activity such as that on page 170, students become familiar with the use of study guides and scripts as aids in understanding these materials. Encourage independent use of the audiovisual collection by interfiling audiovisual cards in the card catalog and setting up a permanent listening and viewing station.

The periodical collection is used as a source of current information not found in books or encyclopedias. Sixth grade students are instructed in using the magazine index to enable them to find articles on specific topics.

As students use the *Abridged Reader's Guide to Periodical Literature*, they will learn that not all of the magazines indexed are in the library media center collection. They will become aware that some indexes lead to materials outside of the collection. This is an opportune time to introduce the concept of library networking and the possibility of interlibrary loan (see the activity "Interlibrary Sources," on page 164).

All of these materials become possible sources of information for research and reporting. Sixth grade students also extend their bibliographic skills. They learn to use footnotes to denote the exact page to find specific information or a quotation. Bibliographies are required for all research and reporting assignments, and footnotes may be included when appropriate.

In these ways, the sixth graders begin to use discrimination in evaluating and selecting the materials available to them. Encourage them to use as wide a variety of resources as possible. A student develops an enduring understanding of the library media center collection by using the materials in a meaningful way.

Reading

Some sixth grade students feel that they have outgrown the fiction collection in the library media center and that there are no longer any books that are of interest to them. There are many excellent books for sixth graders to read for entertainment. These books are transition books that form a bridge between children's literature and adult literature. Sometimes they are referred to as young adult books. There is a tendency not to purchase these books for a collection in an elementary school library media center because only a small percentage of the school population reads them. Not all of the sixth graders will be interested in or ready for this type of book. But transition books more than justify their cost, even though some children don't reach this level until after elementary school. Having a small but good selection of transition books helps to maintain students' interest in reading at this crucial age when permanent tastes and habits are forming. When sixth graders continue to find interesting, challenging materials, they tend to make a smoother transition to using the library media center in the upper school.

Book talks are effective for introducing more challenging materials to sixth graders. Highlight books from the collection that students would rarely be drawn to on their own. Describe sections of the books that relate to the students' current concerns or interests. Choose books that depict problems that the students can relate to or select a popular type of literature that the students are familiar with through television and films.

Provide opportunities for students to recommend books to one another. An activity is included in this section in which the students vote on their favorite books for a best-seller list. Sixth graders are influenced by the opinions of others and seek to follow the examples of group leaders and the majority of peers. Sharing opinions among themselves on books to read is often more successful in stimulating interest in reading than are suggestions made by you or other adults.

Literature Appreciation

In sixth grade, students are given opportunities to analyze the differences between fiction and nonfiction by closely examining the elements of historical fiction and realistic fiction. These types of fiction are based on actual events or true-to-life situations. Initial exposure to this literature is confusing to students, sometimes leading to false conclusions and misconceptions. The activities on pages 171 and 173 develop a clear understanding of these kinds of fiction.

The students are asked to assume the role of an author by writing their own historical fiction and realistic fiction stories. This technique was used in fourth grade with mystery and fantasy and in fifth grade with science fiction and biography. Sixth graders learn the unique characteristics of each kind of fiction and use these elements to write their own stories. In this way, they can appreciate an author's efforts in creating an effective story. They become more proficient at evaluating and selecting what they read.

Audiovisual Production

The technique of having children write to understand, evaluate, and select literature is adapted to nonprint media. Sixth graders can produce their own audiovisual materials for a similar purpose. The students watch a substantial amount of television and listen to hours of radio and recordings. Producing their own audiovisual materials enables them to understand media from the inside. By taking the role of producers, they face problems and make decisions necessary to present ideas in nonprint forms. This increases students' understanding of ideas presented in nonprint media and develops their ability to evaluate and to select materials to listen to and view.

The activity "Audiotaped Interviews," on page 166, gives students the opportunity to make their own nonprint material. The students are directed to:

1. Be familiar with the equipment.
2. Have equipment ready and in good working condition.
3. Develop clearly stated questions.
4. Be polite and friendly.
5. Let the person talk; do not interrupt repeatedly.

By following these guidelines, the students can produce a successful interview on audiotape. The students learn that interviews, unlike casual conversations, are carefully preplanned. In this way, they learn to evaluate televised interviews using different criteria from those used in a one-to-one spontaneous conversation with a friend.

In fifth grade, children learn to make visuals to accompany reports using slides, transparencies, or filmstrips. In the sixth grade, they learn to produce an audiotape. In this way, they learn the elements of audiovisual production, which are combined in the television programs that they view. You may want to introduce videotaping to the students at this time. In this sequence, videotaping is introduced at the advanced level. Once the students have produced audio and visual media separately, the next step is to combine the two into one medium.

Transition

The sixth grade is a transition year. The students are preparing to emerge from the closely supportive group environment of the elementary school library media center into the broader, more independent atmosphere of an upper school library media center. This is the last year that most students will have consistent, close contact with the library media specialist. Although instruction will continue, it will not be on a regularly scheduled basis. It will shift, instead, to an occasional lesson or unit of lessons on a particular tool, concept, or skill. Advanced students will be expected to make extensive independent use of the library media center. This sequence is planned to have the students acquire the basic skills of library media center use by the end of sixth grade.

Summary

Sixth grade is a transition year. Students are preparing for independent, individual use of the upper school library media center. The library and information skills previously learned are reviewed and put into use in research and reporting assignments. By the end of sixth grade, students should be independently able to locate, select, and interpret materials for information and entertainment.

SIXTH GRADE LIBRARY SKILLS
CHECKLIST AND ACTIVITIES

The following presents a sequential checklist of library and information skills to be developed in the sixth grade and suggested activities for teaching specific skills. Each activity is keyed to a major skill objective at the sixth level and is ready for your immediate use or adaptation.

Library Skills Checklist
SIXTH GRADE

Class_____

I. Location Skills

A. Card Catalog

1. Understands that the card catalog is an index to the library media center collection
2. Can locate materials using call numbers on catalog cards
3. Can use the card catalog to locate materials by author, title, and subject

   a. **Alphabetizing**

     (1) Can alphabetize by interior letters of words
     (2) Can interpret drawer labels on the card catalog

   b. **Subject Headings**

     (1) Understands and uses cross-references
     (2) Can convert own terminology into that used in subject headings
     (3) Can be specific when looking up a subject

   c. **Descriptive Information**

     (1) Can interpret information on catalog cards, e.g., type, date, and level of material, whether illustrated
     (2) Can use information on catalog cards to compile a bibliography

B. Fiction and Nonfiction

1. Understands the difference between fiction and nonfiction
2. Knows various kinds of fiction: adventure, science, realistic, mystery, historical, fantasy, sports, humorous
3. Has read some of each of the various types of fiction
4. Can use the nonfiction collection as a source of information

C. Dewey Decimal System

1. Understands the ten main classes
2. Understands that the ten main classes can be divided and subdivided into more specific subjects
3. Understands that the purpose of the system is to pull together materials on the same subject and literary form
4. Can locate materials using call numbers

Class_____

D. Reference Collection
1. Can distinguish the unique characteristics of various reference sources
2. Can determine the reference source most appropriate for a specific purpose

    a. **Encyclopedias**
       (1) Can use cross-references to locate information in an encyclopedia
       (2) Can use indexes to locate information in an encyclopedia

    b. **Dictionaries**
       (1) Can use alphabetical order and guide words in dictionary work
       (2) Can obtain definitions from dictionary entries
       (3) Can use pronunciation keys
       (4) Can use specialized English language dictionaries

    c. **Other Reference Tools**
       (1) Can use almanacs to find statistics and other facts
       (2) Can use atlases to locate places
       (3) Can use biographical dictionaries and geographical dictionaries

E. Biographical Sources
1. Can locate information about a person
2. Knows the different types of biographical materials and can locate information in each
3. Can locate information about a person in the collective biography collection and biographical dictionary

F. Periodicals
1. Is familiar with periodicals of varying scope and purpose
2. Knows periodicals are a source of current information
3. Can interpret citations in *Abridged Reader's Guide to Periodical Literature*

G. Indexes
1. Knows indexes provide access to information by subject in book and reference sources
2. Can locate information on a subject using a book's index
3. Can locate information in an encyclopedia using an index
4. Can interpret citations in *Abridged Reader's Guide to Periodical Literature*
5. Is aware of indexes to information beyond the library media center's immediate collection

Class_____

H. Vertical Files
1. Knows the type of material found in vertical files, e.g., pictures, clippings, pamphlets
2. Can locate vertical file materials for an appropriate purpose

I. Audiovisual Materials and Equipment
1. Knows information comes in a variety of formats
2. Can locate materials in the audiovisual collection
3. Can operate equipment in order to use materials
4. Can produce audiovisual materials to accompany a report

II. Interpretation Skills
A. Evaluation and Selection Techniques
1. Understands the various forms of literature
2. Is acquainted with authors and their works
3. Can select materials for entertainment
4. Can use various parts of a book to determine scope, format, and timeliness, and to locate and document information
5. Is developing discrimination in selecting books and periodicals to read, as well as films and television to view

B. Research and Reporting Techniques
1. Can locate materials to discover what others have found out about a topic
2. Can use ideas gained through different materials
3. Can carry research through to a conclusion
4. Can present information in a written report and/or an oral presentation
5. Can make a bibliography of sources used in a report
6. Understands the function of footnotes

C. Listening and Viewing Skills
1. Attends to the sights and sounds of the instructional situation
2. Interprets what is heard and seen
3. Can recall, summarize, paraphrase, and extend what is listened to and viewed

D. Literature Appreciation
1. Is familiar with various forms of literature
2. Can interpret meaning from many forms of literature

I. LOCATION SKILLS

LOCATION SKILLS REVIEW GAME

This team game provides a comprehensive review of library media center skills that have been learned in grades kindergarten through five. Competitive team games motivate students to review skills.

Time: 30- to 40-minute sessions

Materials: 30 to 50 slips of paper approximately 3″ × 5″
4 pencils

Preparation: Arrange four small desks in a row at one end of the library media center. Equip each desk with some slips of paper and a pencil. Prepare a list of 15 to 20 review questions from the following instructional areas: card catalog, fiction and nonfiction categories, Dewey Decimal System, reference collection, biographical sources, periodicals, indexes. The questions should be able to be answered in a word or short phrase. See the sample list below.

Activity Directions:

Divide the class into two teams by counting off one and two. Choose one student to be scorekeeper. Have one team line up on one side of the library media center and the other team on the opposite side. You may suggest that they take chairs on which to sit.

Call the first two members from each team to the front and have them sit at the desks. Ask a review question requiring a short, one- or two-word answer. Have the four students write their answers on a slip of paper. When they have completed answering the question, have them hold up the papers to show the class and take turns reading their answers.

If both team members have correctly answered, their team is awarded three points. If one team member has the correct answer, his or her team earns one point. A team may be awarded a bonus point if the opposing team holds up the game by talking or exhibiting other undisciplined behavior.

Continue until all team members have had a turn. The team with the most points is the winner.

Follow-up: Play the game repeatedly throughout the year, using different review questions. You might want to concentrate on reviewing one skill area at a time.

The following are examples of review questions:

What kind of information is in magazines? _____

Books about more than one person's life are called _____
_____.

The index to the library media center collection is _____.

Another word for magazines and newspapers is _____.

The three kinds of cards in the card catalog are _____,
_____, and _____.

The numbers and letters on the spine labels of books are the _____ _____.

A good source for an overview of a topic is an_____.

A book of maps is an _____.

To find information in a book on a topic not listed in the table of contents, use the _____.

Topics in encyclopedias are usually arranged _____.

Where is the call number found on a catalog card? _____

I. LOCATION SKILLS   C. Dewey Decimal System

CATEGORY REVIEW

This game reviews Dewey Decimal categories without requiring memorization of corresponding numbers. It offers opportunities for students to practice using the division and subdivision of Dewey categories.

Time: 30 to 40 minutes

Materials: A chart of the ten main categories of the Dewey Decimal system

NOTE: *This game is an extension and variation of a game used in the fifth grade to review subjects included in each Dewey Decimal category.*

Activity Directions:

Have the students group into teams of three or four. Have each team sit in a circle with the members facing each other. Choose one student to be scorekeeper.

Explain that each team will choose one of the ten Dewey Decimal categories and each team member will attempt to name a lower division and subdivision. Have one team demonstrate the following: The first person starts off by snapping the fingers of his or her left hand while saying "Category" and the fingers of his or her right hand while naming a Dewey category. The next person repeats the Dewey category with the left snap and names a subdivision with the right snap. For example: 1. "Category—Science" 2. "Science—Animals" 3. "Animals—Birds" 4. "Birds—Penguins." This is continued until a team member cannot name a further subdivision.

The teams are awarded a point for each term mentioned. The team with the most points wins. A challenge may be made by any member of another team who does not agree with the subdivision named. A challenge is made by quietly raising a hand and waiting until after the team has completed a turn. After the team has finished its turn, provide an opportunity for all challenges to be stated. Challenges may be voted upon by the class or decided by the library media specialist. The scorekeeper records the points, which are derived from the number of divisions named until a challenge has been accepted or a team member cannot name a further subdivision.

Allow five minutes of planning time for each team to choose a category and decide on divisions and subdivisions. Team members may not write down the divisions, but they may coach each other if one is forgotten.

This game usually takes one session to learn, and it stimulates fun and enthusiasm when played thereafter.

Follow-up: This game may be played at various sessions throughout the year.

I. LOCATION SKILLS   D. Reference Collection

THE BIOGRAPHICAL DICTIONARY

This activity provides students with the opportunity to distinguish the unique characteristics of a biographical dictionary so they will be able to determine the most appropriate time to use this source. It also gives practice in locating information in this reference source.

Time: Two 30- to 40-minute sessions and additional individual research time

Materials: 25 to 30 sheets of writing paper

Webster's Biographical Dictionary.
G and C Merriam Co., 1976.

NOTE: *Most library media centers have only one copy of a biographical dictionary. This activity must be completed individually by the students at times other than when the entire class is scheduled to use the library media center.*

Preparation: Select the names of people from the biographical dictionary and write each one at the top of a piece of paper. Have one person for each student in the class.

Activity Directions:

Session I—Have the children discuss the definition of a biographical dictionary. Develop the concept that a dictionary contains the meanings of words and a biographical dictionary has concise biographies of noteworthy persons. Explain that the people included are from past times and that currently popular people will not be in this source. Choose a few people the students would be familiar with and have several students look up and read about the people while others look on.

Give each student a paper with the name of a famous person at the top. Explain that they are to look up the person in the biographical dictionary and find out when they lived and why they were noteworthy. Ask them to be ready to share the information with the class at the next session.

Session II—Provide all students with an opportunity to report on the person assigned to them. Encourage them to describe any problems or unusual items that they encountered when using the dictionary.

Here are some examples of people to locate in the biographical dictionary:

Pizarro
Edgar Allen Poe
Pocahontas

Follow-up: Alert the subject area teachers to the existence of this source and inform them that students are able to use it. Recommend the use of the biographical dictionary in addition to other biographical sources to answer reference questions on people.

I. LOCATION SKILLS   D. Reference Collection

THE GEOGRAPHICAL DICTIONARY

This activity gives students the opportunity to distinguish the unique characteristics of a geographical dictionary so they will be able to determine the most appropriate time to use this source. It also gives practice in locating information in this reference source.

Time: Two 30- to 40-minute sessions and additional individual research time

Materials: 25 to 30 sheets of writing paper

Webster's New Geographical Dictionary.
G and C Merriam Co., 1977.

NOTE: *Most library media centers have only one copy of a geographical dictionary. This activity must be completed individually by the students at times other than when the entire class is scheduled to use the library media center.*

Preparation: Find the names of places in the geographical dictionary and write each one at the top of a piece of paper. Have enough places for each student in the class.

Activity Directions:

Session I—Have the children discuss the definition of a geographical dictionary. Develop the concept that a dictionary contains the meanings of words and that a geographical dictionary contains the names of places with brief geographical and historical information and pronunciation instructions.

Give each student a paper marked with the name of a place at the top. Explain that they are to look up the place in the geographical dictionary and to find out where the place is and as many other facts as the dictionary gives. Ask them to be ready to share the information with the class at the next session.

Session II—Provide all students with an opportunity to report on the place assigned to them. Encourage them to describe any problems or unusual items that they encountered when using the dictionary.

Here are examples of places they can locate in the geographical dictionary:

Muskogee
Golden
Donnybrook

New Harmony
Sweet Water

Follow-up: Alert the teacher of social studies to the existence of this source and to the fact that the students are able to use it. Recommend the use of the geographical dictionary in addition to the atlas to answer reference questions on places.

I. LOCATION SKILLS   D. Reference Collection

ATLASES

This team game reviews the ability to locate places in an atlas.
Time: 30 to 40 minutes
Materials: One atlas for each group of four students
Preparation: Select 20 to 30 names of places from the atlas.
Activity Directions:
Divide the class into teams of four. Give each team an atlas. Have the students compete against each other to see how quickly they can locate places on the maps in the atlases. Remind the students to use the indexes and key instructions to aid them. Provide a few minutes for the students to browse through the atlas to become familiar with its arrangement.

Name a place and write it on the chalkboard. Have the students indicate by raising their hands that they have located the place in the atlas. Ask the first team that is ready to show the class the place on the map and to describe how they located it. Have each of the other teams give the same information. The first team to correctly locate each place wins a point. The team with the most points at the end of the session is the winner.

Variations: The atlases from the library media center collection may vary somewhat in the format and key instructions. After five turns, you might want to switch the atlases that each team is using to locate places.

Follow-up: This game may be repeated using different places to locate.

I. LOCATION SKILLS   D. Reference Collection

ALMANACS

This game involves the students in locating information in almanacs. It provides a review of the scope and arrangement of an almanac.
Time: 30 to 40 minutes
Materials: One almanac for each student in the class:
The World Almanac
1278 West Ninth Street
Cleveland, Ohio 44113

NOTE: *It is easier to learn to use the almanac when each student has a copy. The small print and compact format of the almanac make it difficult to be used by more than one person at a time. Paperback copies are relatively inexpensive and may be shared among the library media specialists in a school district. For the purpose of learning the scope and arrangement of an almanac, it is not necessary that the most current issue be used. The almanacs may be used for instruction for several years.*

Preparation: Select 15 to 25 reference questions from the almanac.

Activity Directions:

Divide the class into four teams and choose a scorekeeper. Give each student an almanac. Briefly review the scope and arrangement of the almanac while the students scan their copies. Call attention to the index in the front and recommend its use for locating information rapidly.

As you read each reference question, have the students locate the answer in the almanac as quickly as possible. Have the students indicate that they have the answer by raising their hands. Note the first hand to go up, but allow time for most of the students to locate the answer before calling on that student. Have the student give the answer and cite the page on which the information was found. Have all of the students turn to the page. If the answer is correct, that team gets a point. If the answer is not correct, call on a member of another team. At the end of the session, the team with the most points wins.

Follow-up: This game may be repeated throughout the year with other reference questions. This activity also provides practice in the use of indexes to locate information.

Reference questions that can be derived from the almanac include the following:

Where was natural gas discovered recently?
How much are U.S. Naval officers paid?
Who is the head of state of the Netherlands?
What is the highest mountain in the U.S.?
What was the favorite television program during the year covered in the almanac?
What percentage of the population has television sets?
Who won the 1960 World Series?
What is the population of your town?
Who was kidnapped on December 8, 1963?

I. LOCATION SKILLS   E. Biographical Sources

"ABOUT THE AUTHOR"

This activity acquaints students with biographical reference sources. Practice is provided in locating information about an author.

Time: Two 30-minute sessions and additional individual research time

Materials: *The Junior Book of Authors*—4 volumes

H. W. Wilson Co.

950 University Avenue

Bronx, New York 10452

Preparation: This activity should be planned in conjunction with a language arts lesson requiring information on authors of children's literature. The language arts curriculum often has a unit on books and their authors. Students may be asked to find information about the life of an author whose work they have read.

Activity Directions:

Session I—Briefly review the definition of biographical dictionaries that describes them as sources of short biographical sketches on noteworthy people in all walks of life. Explain that reference collections usually have special biographical dictionaries of people known for the same type of endeavor, such as presidents, composers, or authors. Show the class *The Junior Book of Authors*.

Choose several students to name an author. Select other students to locate information on the authors in *The Junior Book of Authors*. Have them demonstrate to the class how they located the person and read some of the information cited. Be certain that the students notice the alphabetical arrangement.

Provide time for the students to take turns using *The Junior Book of Authors* to locate information on the author that they have chosen in language arts. Explain that by the next session they should be prepared to tell the class about the author. Additional time should be provided for students to come to the library media center individually to use *The Junior Book of Authors*.

Session II—Have each student report to the class on what they found out about the author.

Variations: If it is not convenient to coordinate this activity with the language arts curriculum, you may have each student choose a book that he or she has enjoyed and look for information on that author. You might list some favorite books and their authors on the chalkboard to give the students ideas.

I. LOCATION SKILLS   F. Periodicals

CURRENT EVENTS

This activity is intended to increase the students' understanding that periodicals are a source of current information. It provides practice in interpreting citations in the *Abridged Reader's Guide to Periodical Literature* and in locating articles in magazines.

Time: Two 40-minute sessions and additional time for small groups to research

Materials: One booklet for each student:
How to Use the Reader's Guide to Periodical Literature
Free from: The H. W. Wilson Company
950 University Avenue
Bronx, New York 10452
or
Back issues of the *Abridged Reader's Guide to Periodical Literature*

Preparation: Coordinate this activity with an assignment from a subject area in the curriculum. The assignment might be to choose one of the current topics or recent events from a list on the chalkboard and to write a paragraph or two to be shared with the class. Gather information from a magazine. Cite the topic, magazine, date of the magazine, and page at the top of the paper.

Activity Directions:

Session I—Have the students consider where they would find information on something that happened recently, something that is too recent to be in books or encyclopedias. Develop the concept that magazines and newspapers are a source of current information and that libraries keep back issues of periodicals for readers to use. Review the definition of the term *periodical.*

Give several examples of high-interest recent events that the students might want to read about. Explain that to find an article on the event they could take a stack of magazines and look through each one. An easier way that saves time is to use an index. Have the students recall when they used an index in a book or an encyclopedia to locate a topic. Draw attention to the alphabetical arrangement by subject of these indexes.

Explain that the *Reader's Guide* is an index used to locate magazine articles. Distribute booklets or back issues. Allow a few minutes to scan the index so the students can find the topics included and the arrangement of subjects. Draw attention to the alphabetical arrangement of the topics. Choose several students to name topics in the index.

Draw attention to the many abbreviations used in the citations. Have the students turn to the page entitled "Abbreviations of Periodicals Indexed." Explain that abbreviations are used to save space. Have the students read through the list and note the magazines that are familiar to them. Choose several students to read the names of favorite magazines and their abbreviations.

Explain that there are other abbreviations used. Have the students turn to the page entitled "Abbreviations." Ask them to find the names of the months. Have several students read the abbreviations for different months. Ask what abbreviation is used to show that a magazine article has a picture. Explain that these keys are to be referred to when they find an unfamiliar abbreviation.

Session II—Distribute the booklets or back issues. Have the students turn to the first page of the index that lists articles. Explain that each item listed is called a citation. Have the students read through the subject headings to determine how they are printed. Draw attention to the boldface type used to indicate subject headings. Next, draw attention to the subheadings, which are printed in the center of the page in smaller boldface type. Have several children give examples of headings and subheadings.

"Briefly review the use of cross-references. Have the students describe how "See" and "See Also" references indicate other subjects to look up for information on a topic.

Read and describe one citation while the students follow in their copies. Explain that the title of the article, the name of the magazine, the page, and the date are cited.

Have each student choose a partner. Explain that each group will read through a citation together and describe it to the class. Have the students turn to the subject "MOTION PICTURE." (If back issues are used choose a subject heading that may be found in all issues of the index, such as "AUTOMO-BILES.") Tell the groups to find the subheading "REVIEWS" and to choose a film from those listed. Have each group prepare to tell the class where they would find an article about the film. Allow 10 minutes to complete the assignment. Provide an opportunity for each group to read the citation and interpret it to the class.

Follow-up: Have students come to the library media center in groups of five to six to locate magazine articles on their chosen topics. Most students will encounter difficulty the first time they look for articles. Give individual assistance and encouragement. The students should understand that they may not find the first article that they look for. Often they will need to substitute another article. Other assignments may be made in subject areas that require students to use information in magazines.

> **NOTE:** *To aid the students in locating articles, select several magazines to keep only for research, such as* Time, Newsweek, *and* U.S. News and World Report. *Keep the back files of these magazines in perfect order. Only the most recent issues should circulate or be kept with the regular library media center collection.*

I. LOCATION SKILLS   G. Indexes

INTERLIBRARY SOURCES

This activity introduces the concept that some indexes direct users to information beyond the library media center collection.

Time: 30 to 40 minutes

Materials: *Abridged Reader's Guide to Periodical Literature,*
                    one back issue for each student
                    Paper
                    Pencils

Activity Directions:
Explain that some indexes list books and periodicals that are not in the library media center collection. Distribute copies of the *Abridged Reader's Guide*. Have the students turn to the page that lists the periodicals indexed. Have them check the magazine collection against the list to find the magazines that are in the collection.

Have the students make two lists, one of magazines indexed that are in the library media center collection and another of magazines not in the collection. Allow 15 minutes to complete the activity. Have the students share what they have found.

Ask them what they would do if they were looking for an article from a magazine that was not in the library media center. Discuss the alternatives. Develop an understanding that they can note the citation and go to a public or university library. Introduce the concept of an interlibrary loan. Explain that research materials can be obtained from another library through an interlibrary loan.

I. LOCATION SKILLS   G. Indexes

INTERPRETING CITATIONS

This activity provides practice in locating information on a subject by using an index. The students are given opportunities to interpret index citations and to locate topics.

Time: Two 30- to 40-minute sessions and additional individual research time

Materials: Paper
Pencils

Preparation: List the topics on a chalkboard so that the students can copy them or put the exercise on a worksheet.

Topics for this exercise include the following:

Bivalve
Canned Food
Duryea Car
Dwarf Star
Float (Parade)
Pollution
Irish Fairy Tales
Supernaturalism
Roaring '20s
Robber Baron

Activity Directions:
Session I—Review the use of indexes by choosing several students to

describe how to find information that is not listed in the table of contents of a book or by alphabetical order in an encyclopedia. Explain that indexes contain references to insignificant facts as well as substantial information. Describe the following: "Sometimes after you have followed an index citation to the correct page, it is difficult to find the topic on that page. There may not be a subheading to direct you to the information. Therefore, you will need to scan the page to find the topic and read the sentence or paragraph referring to the topic to determine whether the information is useful. Some information will be what you need. Other information will not be useful."

Explain that this exercise will help them to scan a page to locate information on a topic to determine whether it is useful for their research. Direct the students to find information on the listed topics in an encyclopedia using an index. Explain that they are seeking information other than that contained in a main article, which is listed alphabetically under the topic. This additional information is included in articles about other topics and is located by using the index.

Have the students locate each topic in an encyclopedia index, write the citation, and briefly note some facts that are found by scanning the page cited. Allow 30 minutes to work on the exercise. Have the students complete the exercise by the next session.

Session II—Give each student an opportunity to share the facts that he or she found. Encourage them all to discuss problems that they encountered in locating information on topics cited in the indexes.

Follow-up: Direct individual students to indexes when additional information on a topic is needed.

Variation: This activity may be adapted to book indexes as well as to encyclopedia indexes.

I. LOCATION SKILLS   I. Audiovisual Materials and Equipment

AUDIOTAPED INTERVIEWS

This activity provides students with an opportunity to produce audiotapes to accompany a report or other subject area study.

Time: Two 30- to 40-minute sessions and additional class time in subject area

Materials: Blank cassette tapes—one for each student
Cassette recorders

Preparation: This is an interview activity that should be coordinated with an assignment in a subject area in the curriculum. The students might be asked to interview a person about his or her opinion of a current news event. The interviews could be used as a basis for class comparison and study. The interview assignment might accompany a written or oral report.

Activity Directions:
Session I—Describe and demonstrate how to operate the cassette recorder to record a blank tape. Have the students choose a partner. Explain that they are going to practice recording interviews in preparation for their assignment. Distribute one cassette recorder and one blank tape to each group.

Explain that there are some steps to a successful interview. Write "Interviewing" on a chalkboard. List the following preparatory steps:

1. Be familiar with the equipment.
2. Have equipment ready and in good working condition.
3. Develop clearly stated questions.
4. Be polite and friendly.
5. Let the person talk; don't interrupt repeatedly.

Briefly discuss the reasons behind each step.

Announce the interview topic and write it on the chalkboard. Choose a debatable issue in the school or community. Have each student develop two questions on the topic. Have the partners take turns interviewing each other.

Session II—Provide an opportunity for each group to play their interviews to the class. Discuss the things that make the interviews either effective or disappointing. You might have the students choose the three to five best interviews and discuss why these were successful.

Follow-up: Assist the teacher in having the students prepare their interviews by writing the questions. Distribute the equipment and provide an opportunity for each student to interview a member of the school community. The teacher may use the recorded interviews for class study and discussion.

Variation: You may want to provide an opportunity for students to interview people outside of the school. A possible assignment is to have them interview an older person in their family or community who could describe an event that took place when that person was young.

II. INTERPRETATION SKILLS   A. Evaluation and Selection Techniques

BEST SELLER NOMINATIONS

This activity develops discrimination in selecting books to read. It stimulates interest in various books and encourages students to read books that others have enjoyed. In this activity students become involved in recommending books to one another.

Time: Two or three 30- to 40-minute sessions
Materials: One piece of oaktag, 24" × 36"
          Marking Pens
Activity Directions:
Sessions I and II—Explain to the students that they are going to have a contest to determine the best sellers for sixth graders in the library media

center collection. Have students nominate books for the best-seller list by giving the title, author, and call number of the book and have them describe their reasons for considering the book a best seller. The students may choose fiction or nonfiction books from the library media center collection. They will probably need two sessions to nominate their favorite books. Keep a chart, listing the books and call numbers as they are nominated. Have the students nominate 20 to 30 titles.

Session III—Read the list of books nominated for the best-seller list. Have the students vote on the nominated best sellers by writing their first choice on a piece of paper. Collect and count the votes. List the top ten choices according to the number of votes received. If two books receive an equal number of votes, list both books as being tied for that place. Entitle the chart "Sixth Grade Best Sellers."

Follow-up: Display the chart in the library media center. Children from other grades also will be interested in reading the books.

II. INTERPRETATION SKILLS   B. Research and Reporting Techniques

INTRODUCING FOOTNOTES

This activity helps students to understand the function of footnotes in a report. The use of footnotes is an extension of the ability to write a bibliography for a report.

Time: 30 to 40 minutes

Materials: Paper
Pencils

Preparation: This activity should be used in conjunction with assigned research and reporting in a subject area.

Activity Directions:

Through a discussion review the reasons for writing a bibliography of sources in a report. Develop the understanding that when the students use published ideas and facts they must give credit to the originator. Ask the students to consider what they would do if they wanted to use the exact wording of an author. Remind them to use quotation marks around material that they quote from a text.

Explain that footnotes are used to show the source of a quotation, idea, or fact. Describe and demonstrate on the chalkboard the way to cite a footnote. Explain that footnotes are numbered consecutively throughout a report. To indicate the first footnote, write a number 1 a half space above the line at the end of the quotation, idea, or fact. Put a corresponding number 1 at the bottom of the page with the author, title, publisher, date, and page number of the source. Explain that the word *footnote* means a note at the foot of a page. At the end of the report, remind the students to remember to cite the source in the bibliography.

Ask the students to explain the difference between a footnote and a bibliography. Develop the concept that footnotes cite the exact location of specific information from a source. The bibliography cites the sources of information generally used in the report as a whole.

Have the students practice writing footnotes by making a sample. Have them choose a nonfiction book and a passage to quote. Copy the quotation and make an appropriate footnote for it. Collect the papers at the end of the session.

Follow-up: Correct the papers to determine which students need further instruction in writing footnotes. Provide individual instruction for those students who need additional help. Make arrangements with the subject area teacher to check footnotes as well as bibliographies included in reports. In this way you may assist those students who have not mastered these skills.

> **NOTE:** *There are other types of footnotes, such as those that amplify a text. These are not considered bibliographic skills and are taught in language arts.*

II. INTERPRETATION SKILLS   B. Research and Reporting Techniques

ALL THE FACTS

This activity provides an opportunity for students to locate materials so they can discover what others have found out about a topic, use ideas gained through different materials, carry research through to a conclusion, and present information in a written report or an oral presentation.

Time: Six 30- to 40-minute sessions and additional individual research and writing time

Materials: Library media center collection
          Paper
          Pencils

Preparation: This activity should be coordinated with a research and reporting assignment in a subject area of the curriculum. The students should have chosen their topics before beginning the activity.

Activity Directions:

Session I—Have the students locate an article in an encyclopedia on their topic and read the article quickly for an overview of the topic. Direct the students to determine five or more subtopics from the overview. Write the subtopics at the top of separate pieces of paper. Set these aside for taking notes at a later session.

Session II—Have the students locate at least three sources of information on their topics. They may use a variety of sources, such as books, magazines, and filmstrips. Encourage the use of the card catalog, the *Reader's Guide to Periodical Literature*, and the reference collection.

Direct each student to write a bibliography of the sources he or she finds.

Sessions III and IV—Have the students read about their topics and look for details about each of the subtopics in the various sources they have identified. Encourage their use of indexes in books to find the specific information they need on their topic. Remind them to use headings and subheadings to find specific information.

Tell the students to take notes about details on the pieces of paper that have the subtopics written at the top. Remind them to include only details that relate directly to that particular subtopic. When students take notes, they have a tendency to simply copy from the text. Searching for details guides them away from copying word for word. Students also have difficulty combining information from several sources. Noting details about subtopics helps students to abstract the information they need from each source and to combine it into a report.

Sessions V and VI—Have the students write their reports from their notes. Remind them of the procedure learned in fifth grade. Direct them to write an introductory sentence for each subtopic and one or two paragraphs about the details they gathered. The subtopics may be arranged in the order they want them to be in the report. Next, have them write an introductory paragraph that describes what the report is about and a closing paragraph that summarizes their information and draws conclusions.

Have the students exchange their papers to be proofread and corrected.

Follow-up: Direct them to make a final copy to be submitted to the subject area teacher. This draft should include a bibliography and any footnotes that are needed.

Variations: This activity may be repeated with different topics and in various subject areas. The students should demonstrate increasing independence in each step of research and reporting.

II. INTERPRETATION SKILLS   C. Listening and Viewing Skills

USING STUDY GUIDES

This activity introduces students to study guides and scripts included in audiovisual materials. It provides an opportunity for students to use and to become familiar with these aids.

Time: Three or four 30- to 40-minute sessions

Materials: Audiovisual materials from the library media center collection
Record players
Cassette players
Filmstrip viewers

Preparation: Select 10 sets of audiovisual materials that include study guides. Choose fiction and nonfiction materials of interest to sixth graders. Set up ten listening and viewing stations in the library media center. Each station should have room for two or three students to use the materials at one time. At each station, have an audiovisual set and the corresponding equipment.

Activity Directions:

Session I—Explain that most audiovisual materials have study guides to help the students learn from the presentation. Have the students choose one of the listening and viewing stations to view the audiovisual materials and to scan the study guide. Ask the students to write the title of the materials and to answer the following question: What does the study guide tell you to do before, during, and after viewing and listening?

Sessions II and III—The students may continue the assignment at other listening and viewing stations. All of the students will not have time to view every one of the audiovisual materials.

Session IV—Provide an opportunity for students to share the information that they gathered about the study guides. Have them discuss the difference between reading the script and listening to and viewing the audiovisual material. Ask why both kinds of information are useful. Develop the concept that audiovisual materials provide a visual image of the subject, whereas print materials offer more in-depth coverage.

Follow-up: Direct students to use study guides and scripts when they use audiovisual materials. Encourage them to use both audiovisual materials and print materials on the same topic.

II. INTERPRETATION SKILLS   D. Literature Appreciation

HISTORICAL FICTION

This activity enables the students to become familiar with historical fiction. The students more fully understand this kind of literature by taking on the author's role to write their own historical fiction stories.

Time: Six 30- to 40-minute sessions

Materials: Filmstrip—*Rifles for Watie* by Harold Keith.
Newbery Award Records, Miller-Brody Productions, 1971.
Adapted from the book published by
Thomas Y. Crowell Co., New York, 1957.

NOTE: *Other historical fiction filmstrips, videotapes, or films may be used.*

Paper
Pencils
Historical fiction from the library media center collection

Preparation: For best results, this activity should be coordinated with social studies lessons. This may be done by having the students write about a period of history they have recently studied.

Select 10 to 20 historical fiction books for a display.

Activity Directions:

Session I—Have the students discuss the definition of historical fiction. Develop the concept that this genre is fiction having characters and a plot set in an authentic period of history.

Display 10 to 20 historical fiction books from various time periods. Give a brief book talk on each book and include a description of the historical setting, the plot, and the main characters. Encourage the students to select one of the books to read.

Sessions II and III—Show the filmstrip *Rifles for Watie*. Prior to viewing the film, ask the students to notice the historical setting of the story.

After the conclusion of the filmstrip discuss the elements of historical fiction that the students recognized. Develop the understanding that historical fiction is set in an authentic time period. The fictional characters depict what the author imagines it would be like to live in that time. Any facts about actual historical persons used in the story must agree with what history tells of their lives. Ask the students to think of a time period to use for the setting of a story they will write during the next session.

Session IV—Have the students name the time period that they have chosen for their stories. Have them read about that time period in an encyclopedia. Recommend that they make notes of interesting events and customs that they might want to include in their story. Have the students picture what it might have been like to live in those times.

Tell the students to develop a story with characters and a plot set in that time period. They may start writing as soon as they have enough background information. Assist students who are having difficulty by encouraging them to talk about the time period and describe what it might have been like to live then.

Session V—Have the students continue to write the historical fiction stories. Write the following instructions on the chalkboard to aid the students in organizing their time:

1. Choose a period of history.
2. Look up the period in an encyclopedia.
3. Read about the period and take notes.
4. Write a story with characters and a plot.

Have the students follow the directions on the chalkboard. Stress that by the end of the session they should have completed the assignments given in the directions.

All stories that are not completed during session V may be completed as homework, or you may wish to give the students an additional session at this point. Those students who have completed their stories may have time for quiet reading.

Session VI—Have the students exchange their stories with a classmate. Allow 10 to 15 minutes for the students to read each other's stories and to recommend any proofreading corrections.

Have a read-around in which each person reads his or her story to the class. Draw the students' attention to the success of the stories that were carefully researched and that used authentic facts on which to base the story.

Follow-up: The students might want to make colorful covers out of construction paper for their stories and to display them in the library media center to be read by members of the school community outside of their own classroom.

II. INTERPRETATION SKILLS   D. Literature Appreciation

REALISTIC FICTION

This activity enables the students to become familiar with realistic fiction. The students can more fully understand this kind of literature by taking on the author's role by writing their own realistic fiction stories.

Time: Six 30- to 40-minute sessions

Materials: Filmstrip—*Julie of the Wolves* by Jean Craighead George. Newbery Award Records, Miller-Brody Productions, 1973, Adapted from the book published by Harper and Row, New York, 1972.

NOTE: *Other realistic fiction filmstrips, videotapes, or films may be substituted.*

Paper

Pencils

Realistic fiction from the library media center collection

Preparation: Select 10 to 20 realistic fiction books for a display.

Activity Directions:

Session I—Have the students discuss the definition of realistic fiction. Encourage them to give examples of realistic fiction that they have read or seen on television. Develop the concept that this is fiction having very lifelike characters, plot, and setting. Explain that this type of fiction often seems so real that it is difficult to think of it as fiction. Realistic fiction usually presents a problem to which the reader or viewer can relate.

Display 10 to 20 realistic fiction books. Give a brief talk on each book, including a description of the main characters and their problem or situation. Encourage the students to select one of the books to read.

Sessions II and III—Show the filmstrip *Julie of the Wolves*. Prior to viewing the filmstrip, ask the students to observe whether they can identify Julie's problem. After viewing the filmstrip, discuss Julie's problem. Ask the students to discuss how they felt Julie handled her problems. Next, have the children consider what makes this story realistic fiction. Ask why it is fiction and not biography.

Session IV—Review the elements of realistic fiction. Develop the concept that realistic fiction has lifelike characters, a plot, and a setting in a problem situation.

Have the students write a realistic fiction story. Assist students who experience difficulty getting started by encouraging them to talk about a problem situation and how it might be worked out. Explain that to write a realistic fictional story they need to put characters into that situation and to have them work through to a solution.

Session V—Have the students continue to write their stories. All stories should be concluded by the following session.

Session VI—Have the students exchange their stories with a classmate. Allow 10 to 15 minutes for the students to read each other's stories and to recommend any proofreading corrections.

Have a read-around in which each person reads his or her story to the class. Draw the students' attention to the success of the stories that present lifelike situations to which they can relate.

VIII. ADVANCED

Understanding the Information Science Approach

At the advanced level, which includes the seventh and eighth grades, the students' library and information skills are expanded to include an understanding of the information science approach to using library media center materials. The information science approach encompasses the concept that the vast and various sources of information in our environment may be organized to enable a person to locate a specific piece of information or a particular material.

The students at this level should have a general understanding of the ways information may be organized and the resource tools available to help locate information. This is acquired through an overview of sources of information, such as periodicals, television, and books, as well as an in-depth use of a variety of resource tools, such as *Reader's Guide, New York Times Index,* and *Current Biography.*

This chapter provides:

- A description of seventh and eighth graders' needs in terms of the library program
- A checklist of library skills to be developed at the advanced level
- Activities for teaching specific skills

ADVANCED PROGRAM

The advanced level is a direct extension of the kindergarten through sixth grade skills sequence. It does not stand alone as a skills program in itself. The skills program gradually builds the students' abilities to locate and to interpret library media center materials beginning at the readiness level and continuing through the sixth grade. In this sequence, the basic skills in using the library media center are learned by the sixth grade.

In the elementary school, the library media specialist usually meets all of the students on a regular basis. Instruction can take place in a consistent way that is meaningful to children. The skills build upon each other in a hierarchical way. Previously learned skills enable children to accomplish more difficult learning tasks. The learning takes place gradually, step by step, until the children are able to independently use the skills to locate and to interpret materials for information and entertainment.

This gradual sequential learning prepares students for the advanced level of library and information skills. The advanced level consists of the independent use of the library media center and an expanded understanding of information science through occasional instruction.

Instruction

Consistent large group instruction is usually neither necessary nor practical at the advanced level. If, however, the students have not followed the program sequentially through grades kindergarten to six and have not mastered the basic skills, you will need to plan further instruction. Adapt some of the activities suggested in the earlier sections to develop the skills on the Advanced Library Skills Checklist on page 184. You may want to instruct students who have not mastered certain library and information skills individually or in small groups.

Basic skills instruction may be difficult at this level. Sometimes students have been bored by lectures about the card catalog and the Dewey Decimal System, and now they tune out at the very mention of the terms. The optimal age to learn library media center location skills is in the fourth and fifth grades. Children at nine and ten usually are interested in the technical aspects of library use. Once this age is past it is more difficult to gain the attention and interest of students. Teaching library skills at this level is similar in some ways to attempting to teach reading after the primary grades.

The skills needed to use the library media center to locate information are best developed through personal interest and a need for specific information. Much of the motivation needed to learn to use the library media center must come from within the student.

The advanced level is planned for students who are twelve years old and older. This age marks the transition from childhood to maturity. The skills and attitudes acquired in earlier years of development carry over into these years and form a foundation on which to build capabilities for adult living.

Students of this age have a desire to assert individuality, but also have a need to conform. There are many choices for students during this time, often made through trial and error, some with unfortunate results. They learn by sometimes painful experience to bear responsibility for their own actions. This is an age of finding their own identity and breaking away from dependence upon parents and other adults.

Students are beginning to seek meaning and direction in their own lives. Many find little of what they have learned in school of significance to themselves. These students can become resigned to doing assignments because it is required and not because the learning is meaningful to them.

The concepts and skills in the advanced section are planned to be meaningful to students' lives both at the present time and for the future. The activities in this section provide students with opportunities to use materials that can help them to understand and to relate to their environment. The information science approach to library and information skills instruction offers students an overview of information resources and opportunities to select materials that are relevant to them.

Coordination with Subject Areas

The upper school library media center program is dependent upon the students' assignments in subject areas. In this way it is completely coordinated with the curriculum. Students are rarely assigned to the library media center for an instructional session except through a subject area teacher.

The teacher and the library media specialist jointly plan and schedule instruction of specific tools and advanced concepts. It is important for you to be aware of the nature and content of assignments. You can make helpful suggestions to teachers about the resources that are available in the library media center and the skills that the students have acquired.

The emphasis at this level is on independent, individual use of the library media center and an occasional class session for learning to use a specific tool or concept. The activities in this section are planned to be built around an assignment in a subject area. These activities are sufficiently flexible to accommodate a wide variety of assignments that require the use of a specific library media center resource or concept. For example, many different assignments may be given that require students to use *The New York Times Index, Current Biography,* or Bartlett's *Familiar Quotations.*

The instruction in the use of these sources should always be in conjunction with an assignment requiring their use. Students generally learn better through the personal experience of using a resource than they do through listening to a lecture about the resource. Although the explanation of the resource is a useful introduction, it cannot take the place of a hands-on experience. Students will be more able to recall and to transfer what they have learned firsthand.

Information Science Approach

The information science approach is concerned with the collection, organization, retrieval, interpretation, and use of information. The vast amount of information generated in our current society makes the general concepts and concerns of information science important for the library user to understand. The information science approach views library and information skills from a broad perspective that places the library in the context of various sources of information available to the person. This approach reveals the interweaving of these sources to form a network in which the library plays a central and crucial role. The library provides opportunities for people to make use of and to find meaning in the masses of information available to them.

The advanced library and information skills program consists of sources of information and explanations of ways to organize and to use information. The following areas form the major part of the program: computers, Library of Congress cataloging, television, networking of library services, and research and reporting techniques.

Use of Computers

Computers play an increasingly important role in organizing and retrieving information. In the activity "The Computer File," on page 187, students learn that computers may serve the same function as the card catalog. They learn the difference between data retrieval and document retrieval. Students are asked to compare the operations of a computer with the various location tools of the library media center, such as indexes to locate information in books and the card catalog to locate materials. The students are made aware of the necessity to translate their terminology into the language of the computer, a process that is similar to using subject headings and call numbers to locate materials in the library media center.

Library of Congress Cataloging

At an earlier stage in the library and information skills sequence, the Dewey Decimal System was presented as one way to organize materials so that a particular source could be located. The Dewey Decimal System is one of many possible classification systems. By studying it, a model for the way a classification system functions is provided and a way of organizing information is given. At the advanced level, some students begin to use larger libraries for certain research and reporting projects. At this time, it is helpful to introduce the Library of Congress (LC) classification system. There is no need for students to memorize or to thoroughly analyze the mechanics of LC cataloging. Once they have thoroughly analyzed one system, they should be able to quickly adapt to other systems. The activity "Library of Congress Cataloging," on page 190, has students compare LC categories with the familiar Dewey categories to assist them in adapting to other systems. They should become aware that the same procedure is used in locating materials in both types of classification systems. They need to follow the familiar pattern of locating the call number through the card catalog and following labels and other instructions to locate the desired material on the shelf.

Indexes That Lead to Network Services

At the advanced level, indexes that lead students to materials outside of the library media center collection are introduced. Some of the magazines indexed in the *Reader's Guide* will not be included in the library media center collection. Not all of the books indexed in the *Short Story Index, Play Index,* and *Granger's Index to Poetry* will be in the library media center collection.

The networking of library services, which enables students to borrow materials from library collections outside of the library media center, may be introduced at this time. Students can become aware of the relationship of the libraries within the networking system and the provision for cooperative-borrowing privileges, which increase the amount of materials available to them.

Television as a Source of Information

Television is one of the most powerful sources of information in the students' environment. It influences attitudes while providing information and entertainment. The central function of television programming is, of course, to entice people to watch. Attention in itself often becomes the first consideration of programming, while content and purpose lag behind. Evaluation and selection techniques learned in the library media center program may better equip the student to choose programs.

The series of activities entitled "Videotape News Report," on page 197, has a group of students produce a videotape of school news. The students take the roles of director, reporters, scriptwriters, and technicians to plan, produce, edit, and show a television program. In this way they become aware of the internal operations of television programming and can more completely understand and assess what they view. This technique was used in earlier grades by having children write various kinds of fiction to learn the unique characteristics of each from the inside. Just as the child took the role of an author, the student can take the role of a producer to understand from the inside what is viewed. For example, a student who videotapes a baseball game chooses certain shots to emphasize particular action on the field. Later, when he or she views the tape in the studio, few can miss the selected view of the game that is portrayed. Students become aware that viewing a game on television is an entirely different experience from seeing the game at the playing field. This concept and many others that the students begin to experience firsthand enable them to use discrimination in evaluating and selecting materials to listen to and view.

This is an excellent experience for all students to have. You may find, however, that it is not possible to provide all students with an opportunity to produce their own videotapes. The suggested activity involves producing a monthly program of videotaped school news. By having a different group of students producing the program each month, you will be able to offer the opportunity to many of the students. You may find, however, that this is too ambitious at first, and prefer to form a club using the same students for each production.

At the advanced level, students learn that television programs may be extended by using library media center materials. An informational program often introduces ideas and concepts that may be further studied through materials in the library media center. The pacing of television is often more rapid than an individual's thought. A viewer cannot go back over a point that is not fully comprehended. Print materials, while presenting in-depth coverage of topics, also may be paced at the rate of an individual's thought. You can encourage students to follow their inclinations in wanting to know more about a topic by making them aware of related library media center materials. The activity "TV Materials," on page 204, combines a book talk with a display on materials related to recent television programs. The display of television-related materials may be made a permanent part of the library media center by frequently changing the materials to keep them current.

One of the major problems with extensive television viewing is the lack of opportunity it offers to talk about what is seen. Opportunities to discuss television programs develop discrimination in evaluating and selecting programs to watch. In group discussions, students are given opportunities to recall, to summarize, to paraphrase, and to extend what they view. Recalling requires the students to remember what was significant to them. In summarizing, the students gather their thoughts into a manageable form. Paraphrasing requires that they restate what is recalled and summarized in their own words. In extending, the student brings his or her own thoughts and opinions to the ideas presented, as well as some of the information gathered from other sources. People make sense out of their world by relating new experiences and information to past experiences and learning. A group discussion about viewing television helps students to relate what they see to past experience. Through a discussion, they may find that some television programs have little meaning for them. In this way, students can more fully understand and evaluate their television viewing and select more meaningful programs.

Research and Reporting Techniques

Between the ages of twelve and sixteen, most students reach the final stage of mental development, in which they are able to generalize and to deal with abstractions. These are important abilities in research and reporting. The ability to generalize frees the person from the restriction of thinking of specific items and enables a person to group similar items. This ability begins to develop much earlier, enabling children to categorize and to understand library media center classification.

At the advanced level, increased abilities to generalize enable a student to form a hypothesis or otherwise to narrow a topic. This is one of the most difficult techniques in the process of research and reporting. Defining and narrowing a topic may determine the success or failure of the entire project.

Students usually have chosen topics within the subject area before coming to the library media center to gather information. Be alert to topics that are bound to fail because they are too broad or vague. You can be helpful to students on an individual basis by warning them of unmanageable topics and by assisting them to redefine what they will research.

The ability to deal with abstractions is also essential to successful research and reporting. Younger children have a concrete image of what they express. Increased ability to use abstraction means an ability to have thoughts that do not always have a concrete counterpart. A full understanding of many attitudes, such as pride, loyalty, and compassion, requires abstract thinking.

There is another aspect of abstraction that is even more significant to research and reporting. Abstraction includes the ability to select what is important, or what relates to a topic, from a mass of information. The mass of information may be from a variety or sources in different formats. Abstraction further includes the ability to combine information from many sources into one cohesive report.

At the advanced level, students are instructed in report-writing within a subject area. As with narrowing topics, you are in a position to notice students who are experiencing difficulty. Combining sources of information is not a simple task and requires maturity, skill, and experience. Encourage and assist individual students who need help.

Reference Sources

The reference sources introduced through the activities in this section for the advanced level have been chosen for their usefulness in both research and entertainment. These are sources that students will find personally interesting as well as helpful for research. *Current Biography* is enjoyable reading while it also provides useful information about newsworthy people. The use of Bartlett's *Familiar Quotations* and the indexes to short stories, plays, and poetry makes the individual aware of resources for personal use as well as assigned research. Indexes to magazines and newspapers fall into this category also. The vertical file is another source of current high-interest material. These library media center materials are resources that students may use to gather information throughout their lives. They are sources of information to extend other experiences and are interesting in themselves.

Through the activities that introduce these sources, on page 192, the students are given opportunities to become accustomed to a variety of indexing procedures and to various arrangements of reference tools. In this way, they are prepared to adapt these skills to using other special subject reference sources needed for researching in subject areas.

There are other sources in the library reference collection that you will probably want to introduce in relation to specific assignments in a subject area, such as sources of literary criticism, social science dictionaries and encyclopedias, and pure science reference materials. The students may be made aware of the existence of a particular reference source and given a brief description of the arrangement at the beginning of an assignment in which the source may be useful. This should be sufficient to get students to use the source on their own and to adapt skills acquired in using other reference sources.

Literature Appreciation and Reading

At the advanced level, literature appreciation is included in the language arts curriculum. The library media center program does, however, include activities that encourage reading for entertainment and the use of materials for personal interest.

Book talks are an excellent way of making students aware of interesting books in the collection that might otherwise be overlooked. The upper school library media center has a collection of young adult fiction that might be unfamiliar to the students.

You might use three types of book talks: the formal, the informal, and the book fair. The formal book talk consists of a detailed description of one book, including excerpts. The informal book talk consists of a discussion of three or four books that are structured around one theme or one author. The book fair consists of a brief one- or two-sentence description of a large number of books.

The activity "TV Materials," on page 204, includes a book fair of materials related to recent television programs. Book talks can be arduous to prepare. The advantage of the book fair is that it tends to take less time to prepare, while it introduces a wider range of materials. Once you have prepared a book talk, use it with many groups of students to get the full benefit of your effort.

Summary

The advanced level of library and information skills instruction is a continuation and extension of skills learned from the readiness level through the sixth grade. The advanced skills are not meant to stand alone as a complete skills program.

The activities at this level are intended to make students aware of the information science approach to library media center use. At the advanced level, students are introduced to other classification systems, to the use of computers in information management, and to the indexing of sources that lead to materials outside of the library media center collection. They become more fully aware of television as a source of information and are encouraged to use library media center materials to extend television programs. They become familiar with reference sources that are useful for research and are also sources of personally interesting information. Research and reporting for subject areas of the curriculum become the main uses of the library media center.

Advanced level library and information skills are intended to be life-enriching skills for use in both instructional situations and personal pursuits.

ADVANCED LIBRARY SKILLS CHECKLIST AND ACTIVITIES

The following presents a sequential checklist of library and information skills to be developed at the seventh and eighth grade levels and suggested activities for teaching specific skills. Each activity is keyed to a major skill objective at this level and is ready for your immediate use or adaptation.

Library Skills Checklist
ADVANCED LEVEL

Class_____

I.   Location Skills
A.   Card Catalog
1. Understands that the card catalog is an index to the library media center collection
2. Can locate materials using call numbers on catalog cards
3. Can use the card catalog to locate materials by author, title, and subject

   a. **Alphabetizing**

   (1) Can alphabetize by interior letters of words
   (2) Can interpret drawer labels

   b. **Subject Headings**

   (1) Can convert terminology into that used in subject headings
   (2) Can be specific when looking up a subject
   (3) Can use cross-references

   c. **Descriptive Information**

   (1) Can interpret information on catalog cards, e.g., type of material, level of material, how recently published, whether illustrated
   (2) Can use information on catalog cards to compile a bibliography
   (3) Knows a computer may serve the same function as the card catalog

B.   Fiction and Nonfiction
1. Understands the difference between fiction and nonfiction
2. Knows various kinds of fiction: adventure, science, realistic, mystery, historical, fantasy, sports, humorous
3. Has read some of each of the various types of fiction
4. Can use the nonfiction collection as a source of information

C.   Dewey Decimal System
1. Understands the purpose of the system is to pull together materials on the same subject and literary form
2. Understands the ten main classes
3. Understands that the ten main classes can be divided and subdivided into more specific subjects
4. Can locate materials using call numbers
5. Knows that Library of Congress cataloging is used in university and other large libraries

Class_____

D. Reference Collection

1. Can distinguish the unique characteristics of each reference source
2. Can determine the reference tool most appropriate for a specific purpose
3. Knows reference sources are meant to be referred to, not read through
4. Can locate information in reference sources

E. Biographical Sources

1. Can locate information about a person
2. Knows the different types of biographical materials and can locate information in each

F. Periodicals

1. Is familiar with periodicals of varying scope and purpose
2. Understands periodicals are a source of current information
3. Can interpret citations in *Reader's Guide to Periodical Literature*
4. Is familiar with periodicals on microfilm or fiche
5. Can interpret citations in *New York Times Index*

G. Indexes

1. Knows indexes provide access to information by subject in book and reference sources
2. Can locate information on a subject using a book's index
3. Can locate information in an encyclopedia using an index
4. Is aware of indexes to information beyond the library media center's immediate collection
5. Can locate information in periodicals using indexes

H. Vertical Files

1. Knows the type of material found in vertical files, e.g., pictures, clippings, pamphlets
2. Can locate vertical file materials for an appropriate purpose

I. Audiovisual Materials and Equipment

1. Knows information comes in a variety of formats
2. Can locate materials in the audiovisual collection
3. Can operate equipment in order to use materials
4. Can produce own audiovisual materials to express ideas

Class_____

II. Interpretation Skills

A. Evaluation and Selection Techniques
1. Understands the various forms of literature
2. Is acquainted with authors and their works
3. Can use various parts of a book to determine scope, format, and timeliness, also to locate and document information
4. Uses discrimination in selecting books and periodicals to read, films and television to view

B. Research and Reporting Techniques
1. Can locate materials to discover what others have found out about a topic
2. Can use ideas gained through different materials
3. Can carry research through to a conclusion
4. Can present information in a written report and/or an oral presentation
5. Can make a bibliography of sources used in a report
6. Understands the function of footnotes

C. Listening and Viewing Skills
1. Attends to the sights and sounds of the instructional situation
2. Interprets what is heard and seen
3. Can recall, summarize, paraphrase, and extend what is listened to and viewed

D. Literature Appreciation
1. Is familiar with various forms of literature
2. Can interpret meaning from many forms of literature

I. LOCATION SKILLS   A. Card Catalog

THE COMPUTER FILE

This activity introduces the concept that a computer may serve the same function as the card catalog. Students are asked to compare the manual card catalog file with an automatic computer file. They are encouraged to notice the use of computers in information science.

Time: Two 40-minute sessions

Materials: Bulletin board
                 Duplicated sheet of computer terms

Preparation: Prepare and duplicate a handout of computer terms. (See a sample handout following the activity directions.)

Activity Directions:

Session I—Introduce the term *information science* and ask the students to define it through a discussion. Develop the concept that information science is concerned with the collection, organization, retrieval, interpretation, and use of information. Ask the students to discuss why this is important in our current society. Develop an awareness of the vast amount of information continually being generated. Have students give examples of information sources in their environment, such as television, newspapers, magazines, and books. Ask them to name some of the ways the library media center in the upper school is able to keep more materials and information such as microfilm and microfiche than the elementary school library media center.

Explain that computers are used to help control information and materials. Write the following on a chalkboard:

1. Computers are used to store large amounts of information in a small space.
2. Computers are used to locate information rapidly and accurately.

Have the students think about the second use of computers. Ask them how they would find a book on a certain topic in the library media center. Choose several students to describe the steps in using the card catalog to locate a book. Explain that when a computer is used for this purpose it is called *document retrieval*. Have the students discuss how a computer could be used in place of the card catalog. Have them consider the advantages and disadvantages.

Ask the students, "If you needed specific information on a topic, how would you locate that information in the library media center?" Choose several students to describe the use of indexes in the backs of books. Explain that when a computer is used for this purpose it is called *data retrieval*. Have the students discuss how a computer could be used in place of an index. Have them consider the advantages and disadvantages.

Ask the students what problems they sometimes encounter in using subject headings in the card catalog and indexes. Develop the concept through discussions and examples that their language and the terms used in the catalog or index may not be the same. Explain that this is also a problem in using computers. When using a computer, a person uses his or her own language, which must be translated into the computer's language.

Distribute the sheet on computer terms and definitions. Discuss briefly the different types of input and output devices. Provide an opportunity for the students to describe computers that they are familiar with and have used. Develop an awareness of using a videoterminal with a keyboard and of the capability of some computers to react to the human voice or a light pen. Briefly define batch processing and on-line access. Discuss the advantage of using on-line retrieval to provide immediate, direct access to the computer over waiting to use the computer for days or weeks in a batch-processing system.

Ask the students to bring in clippings from newspapers and magazines that describe the use of computers in information storage and retrieval.

Session II—Provide an opportunity for the students to share and to discuss the clippings. Have each student explain the use of the computer as described in the article he or she found. Encourage the other students to ask questions and to discuss each article.

Follow-up: Display the clippings on a bulletin board. You might use the title, "Computers Work for You." Continue to add new clippings to the collection throughout the year.

Variations: You might want to divide the first session into two sessions, depending upon the amount of discussion and participation generated by the students.

Background Source: *An Introduction to Computers in Information Science* by Susan Artandi. Metuchen, N.J.: Scarecrow Press, 1972.

COMPUTER TERMS AND DEFINITIONS

Document retrieval—Location of materials through the computer.

Data retrieval—Location of a specific piece of information through a computer.

Index language—Subject headings, terms, and codes used to classify information and materials.

Hardware—Computer equipment.

Software—Programs that are stored in the computer.

Input—The information put into the computer.

Output—The information provided by the computer.

On-line retrieval—Direct immediate access to the computer by the user.

Batch processing—A task or question that is submitted to a computer operator to be processed and returned to the user at a later time.

Videoterminal—A cathode tube or video screen that shows the information provided by the computer.

Keyboard—A typewriting device that allows the user to communicate with the computer.

Voice recognition—The capability of the computer to react to the human voice.

Light pen—A device used to write on a video screen to enter information into a computer.

I. LOCATION SKILLS   C.   Dewey Decimal System

LIBRARY OF CONGRESS CATALOGING

This activity introduces Library of Congress cataloging and helps students to be aware that it is the classification system used in university libraries and other large libraries. The students become acquainted with the code by comparing it to the more familiar Dewey Decimal System.

Time: Two 40-minute sessions

Materials: Library media center collection
                 Worksheets

Preparation: Prepare and duplicate a list of the main categories in the Library of Congress cataloging. Leave a blank column to fill in the corresponding Dewey Decimal number. (See a sample page following the activity directions.)

Activity Directions:

Session I—Explain that some students may want to use the university library for researching reports. Remind them that the Dewey Decimal System is not the only way to organize and classify materials. Larger libraries use the Library of Congress system of cataloging. Explain that the system is referred to as *LC* and can be subdivided into more precise categories than those of the Dewey Decimal System.

Distribute the worksheets. Have several students read through the categories while the others follow. Explain that the major classes are indicated by letters rather than numbers. Each class may be subdivided by other letters of the alphabet followed by numbers. For example, the LC classification number of a book on games might be GV1201. LC cataloging provides a wider range of call numbers in each category than the Dewey Decimal System; therefore it can accommodate a large collection of materials with precise call numbers.

Direct the students to complete the worksheets by filling in the Dewey Decimal number that corresponds to each LC category. Explain that they may use the library media center collection and the card catalog. Use the rest of the session to complete the assignment. Collect the worksheets at the end of the session.

Session II—Redistribute the corrected worksheets. Have the students go over each category. Answer the questions that the students have. Explain that they do not need to memorize the LC categories to use materials in a large library. Ask students to share any experiences that they have had locating materials in a library classified by LC cataloging. Develop the understanding that the card catalog is used to find the call number and that materials are located by following posted labels and instructions. Point out that they follow the same procedure in other classification systems as they do in locating materials in the library media center by the Dewey Decimal System.

Follow-up: You might plan a field trip to a nearby library that uses LC cataloging to provide students with a firsthand experience. Encourage students to use larger libraries when appropriate.

LC Cataloging	Main Categories	Dewey Decimal System
A	Generalities	_____
B	Philosophy—Religion	_____
C-F	History	_____
G	Geography	_____
H	Social Science	_____
J	Political Science	_____
K	Law	_____
L	Education	_____
M	Music	_____
N	Fine Arts	_____
P	Language—Literature	_____
Q	Science	_____
R	Medicine	_____
S	Agriculture	_____
T	Technology	_____
U	Military Science	_____
V	Naval Science	_____
Z	Bibliography	_____

I. LOCATION SKILLS   D. Reference Collection

BOOKS OF QUOTATIONS

This activity introduces books of quotations as a reference source. Students are given the opportunity to locate a specific quotation.

Time: 40 minutes and individual research time

Materials: *Familiar Quotations* by John Bartlett. Boston: Little Brown, 1968.

Preparation: This activity should be coordinated with an assignment in language arts. The assignment might be to choose a quotation from a list compiled by the teacher and to be prepared to report the source of the quotation and any other facts that you can find.

Activity Directions:

Introduce Bartlett's *Familiar Quotations.* Explain that it is a collection of famous sayings or excerpts of writings of English and American authors and other sources, some dating back to 2000 B.C. Describe the thoroughness of the index, which lists many quotations by a single word. Explain that the index is the key to the quotations, which are listed chronologically by author. Direct the students to locate their quotation in the index and to follow the citation given to the author list.

Choose several students to locate their quotations while the others observe. Encourage students to ask questions about the procedure.

Introduce any other books of quotations in the library media center reference collection.

Follow-up: Provide individual research time for students to use Bartlett's *Familiar Quotations.* Assist students who experience difficulty.

I. LOCATION SKILLS   E. Biographical Sources

CONTEMPORARY NOTABLES

This activity introduces biographical reference sources on contemporary noteworthy persons. It provides an opportunity for students to locate information in *Current Biography* and to become acquainted with *Who's Who, Contemporary Authors,* and other special subject biographical reference sources in the library media center collection.

Time: 40 minutes and additional individual research time

Materials: *Current Biography.* New York: Wilson.

Who's Who. Chicago: Marquis.

Contemporary Authors. Detroit: Gale Research.

Other sources of contemporary biographies in the library media center collection

Preparation: This activity should be coordinated with an assignment in a subject area of the curriculum. The assignment might be to choose a person who, within the past 10 years, has been well-known for an entertainment or recreational contribution. Write an essay describing the person's career. The students should have chosen a person to research prior to the activity.

Activity Directions:

Explain that there are sources in the reference collection that give biographical information on the lives of contemporary persons. Introduce *Current Biography* and point out that it contains sketches of persons of many nationalities who are newsworthy. Explain that it appears monthly and cumulates into annual volumes. Also explain that it is indexed so that information on a person may be located by consulting only four indexes.

Choose several students to locate a biographical sketch while the others observe. Encourage students to ask questions about the procedure.

Explain that there are other sources of contemporary biographies. Briefly introduce *Who's Who, Contemporary Authors,* and any other biographical sources in the library media center reference collection with contemporary information.

Follow-up: Provide time for students to individually locate biographical information on the person they chose. Assist students who experience difficulty.

I. LOCATION SKILLS   F. Periodicals

SOURCES ON MICROFILM

This activity introduces students to periodicals in the library media center collection that are on microfilm and microfiche. It also extends understanding of the *Abridged Reader's Guide* to the more inclusive *Reader's Guide to Periodical Literature.*

Time: Two 40-minute sessions

Materials: *Reader's Guide to Periodical Literature*—one back issue for each student

Library media center magazine collection, including microfilm and microfiche

Duplicated worksheets

Preparation: Prepare and duplicate worksheets with three columns using the following headings.

1. Magazines in back files
2. Magazines on microfilm
3. Magazines not in the collection

Activity Directions:

Session I—Review the uses of the periodical collection as a source of current detailed information not found in books. Draw attention to the variety of special interests that magazines cover. Have the students give examples of magazines that cover a specific subject.

Distribute back issues of the *Reader's Guide to Periodical Literature*. Tell the students to read several citations to themselves and raise their hand if they need assistance with any part of the citation. Individually assist those needing help. If many students are confused about the information presented in the citations, have several students read citations and explain them to the class. Remind the students to refer to the abbreviation keys at the front of each guide.

Tell the students that some of the magazine collection is on microfilm. Explain that microfilm keeps back files intact and also saves storage space. Tell the students that the back issues of other magazines are filed in boxes in the order of the issuing date and arranged in alphabetical order by the title of the magazine. Explain that the *Reader's Guide to Periodical Literature* indexes some magazines that the library media center does not have.

Have the students turn to the list of magazines indexed in their copy of the *Reader's Guide*. Distribute the duplicated worksheet. Explain that they are to determine the column on the worksheet that each magazine on the list in the *Reader's Guide* would fit.

Let the students use the rest of the session to complete the worksheet. Collect the worksheets at the end of the session.

Session II—Distribute the worksheets and provide sufficient time for all students to complete the assignment.

Go over the worksheet by having the students read the titles of the magazines that fit into each column and identify those that are stored in back files, those on microfilm, or those not in the collection.

Ask the students how they could use magazines that are not in the library media center collection. Develop the concept that they can make a note of the citation and look for it in a public or university library. Discuss the possibility of obtaining the magazine through an interlibrary loan.

Follow-up: This activity should immediately precede an assignment in a subject area requiring students to use the periodical collection.

I. LOCATION SKILLS   F. Periodicals

NEWSPAPER INDEXES

This activity introduces indexes to locate information in newspapers. The students are given opportunities to locate articles using the *New York Times Index*. This activity also helps students to understand the difference between primary and secondary sources.

Time: One 40-minute session and individual research time
Materials: *New York Times Index*
New York Times on microfilm
Preparation: This activity should be coordinated with an assignment in social studies. The assignment could be to choose a particular event that took place in the first 50 years of the twentieth century. Find an article about the event in a newspaper and locate information on the same event in a book. Compare the way the event is described in the two sources. The students should have chosen their topics prior to the activity.

Activity Directions:

Through a discussion, define *primary sources* and *secondary sources*. Develop the concept that primary sources are firsthand accounts of an event, whereas secondary sources are a retelling of the event by an author who has researched the topic. Have the students describe some of the differences in the type of information that might be in each source. Explain that their assignment will help them to see the differences more clearly.

Ask the students what would be a source of primary information. Develop the concept that a newspaper reports events at the time that they occur, and often give firsthand accounts. In many instances, newspapers are the closest thing to a primary source you will be able to find.

Describe how to use the *New York Times Index* to locate the reporting of an event. Draw attention to the chronological arrangement as well as to the alphabetical arrangement of subjects. Have several students locate their topics while the others watch. Discuss any problem that the students encounter.

Have one of the students who located a citation on his or her topic find the corresponding microfilm. Demonstrate and describe how to operate the microfilm reader. Have several students take turns operating the reader while the others observe.

Briefly review how to locate nonfiction books on specific events. Remind the students to use indexes in the backs of books to locate specific information. Have the students locate, select, and borrow books on their topics.

Follow-up: Have small groups of students or individuals come to the library media center to use the index to locate newspaper articles on their events and to use the microfilm. Assist students who experience difficulty.

I. LOCATION SKILLS   G. Indexes

SHORT STORY INDEX

This activity introduces indexes as sources for locating short stories, poems, and plays. It helps students to understand that not all indexed materials are in the library media center collection. The activity also makes students aware of library networking services, such as interlibrary loans.

Time: One 40-minute session and additional individual research time

Materials: *Short Story Index* and Supplements
New York: Wilson.

Preparation: This activity should be coordinated with an assignment in language arts. The assignment might be to locate three short stories by the same author and to write an essay comparing the themes, character development, and settings of each.

Activity Directions:

Ask the students to give examples of when they have used indexes. Have them recall locating information in indexes by subject. Introduce the *Short Story Index* and explain that short stories are listed by author and title as well as by subject, as in the card catalog.

Ask the students why short stories are more difficult to locate than books. Develop the understanding that short stories are usually part of a collection, that the title of the book is not the same as the title of the short story, and that collections may include stories written by many different authors. Explain that the *Short Story Index* will name the title of the book that the short story is in. The students may then check the card catalog to determine if the book is in the library media center.

Explain that the short stories indexed in the *Short Story Index* will be in the collections of most large libraries. The library media center, however, may not have all of the books. Ask the students how they might locate a short story that is not in the library media center collection. Develop the understanding that they may make a note of the book containing the short story, and check the collection of a larger library, such as a public library or a university library. You might want to arrange for an interlibrary loan with a large library in the vicinity.

Have the students locate the short stories by taking turns to use the index. Assist students individually if they are experiencing difficulty.

Follow-up: Students will probably need additional time to locate the short stories. Provide assistance as students use the *Short Story Index* during individual research time.

Variation: This activity may be used to introduce the following indexes:

Play Index.
New York: Wilson.

Granger's Index to Poetry.
New York: Columbia University Press.

An assignment in language arts should be coordinated with the introduction of each index.

I. LOCATION SKILLS   H. Vertical Files

TREASURE HUNT

This "treasure hunt" provides an opportunity for students to discover the types of materials in vertical files, such as clippings, pictures, pamphlets, and maps.

Time: 40 minutes

Materials: The vertical file collection in the library media center
                 Paper
                 Pencils

Activity Directions:

Divide the class into four teams. Explain that the vertical file is a source of information that is not listed in the card catalog except for an occasional cross-reference. Explain that they will compete in a treasure hunt of the vertical file materials. Tell each team to survey the vertical files and to list both the various topics covered and the types of materials that they find. Allow the teams 10 minutes to survey the vertical files. Have each team read their list. The team with the most items listed is the winner of the treasure hunt.

Ask the students to give examples of when this material might be useful to them. Develop the understanding that this material is a source of current information not available in books. Point out that these are free materials and discuss the possibility of bias and slanted viewpoints.

Follow-up: Encourage students to use vertical file materials when they are seeking current information.

Variation: You may make up specific reference questions from vertical file materials to have the students answer during the treasure hunt. Vertical file materials vary greatly in each library media center. Reference questions will need to be prepared from the vertical file materials available.

I. LOCATION SKILLS   I. Audiovisual Materials and Equipment

VIDEOTAPE NEWS REPORT

This activity enables students to express ideas through producing their own audiovisual materials. It provides opportunities to use videotape to report on school activities. Students develop a deeper understanding of the medium of television by producing videotapes.

Time: Six 40-minute sessions and additional individual time

Materials: Portable videocamera and recorder
                 Videotapes
                 Monitor and connector cables
                 Additional videotape deck
                 Materials for graphics—poster paper and marking pens

Preparation: This activity is planned for a group of 21 students. You may provide the opportunity for many students by having a different group participate each month. You may prefer, however, to form a video club with the same members throughout the year.

Activity Directions:

Session I—Demonstrate and describe how to use the portable video camera for taping. Explain that the function of the lens is to control the light entering the camera and to focus the picture. The ring closest to the camera controls the light. The ring farthest from the camera controls the focus. Between these two rings is the zoom, which is used for closeup. When videotaping, use the zoom sparingly. You will need to refocus each time you use the zoom. Warn the students to center the picture carefully since the picture that you see in the viewfinder shows more than what will show on the television screen. Caution the students to remember that an effective videotape is simple and that it shows a minimum amount of unrelated material.

Have each student work with a partner, one to use the camera and the other to operate the recorder. Have each group take a turn to videotape, while the others watch. Have the students follow these steps.

1. Check that the camera and sound are working.
2. Find and focus the picture in the viewfinder.
3. Hold the camera steady and avoid sudden movement.

Session II—Explain that the students will be videotaping school activities during the month to show as a school news program. Write the following production tasks on a chalkboard and describe the responsibilities of each:

Director

Scriptwriter

Talent or reporter

Graphic artist

Audio person

Camera person

Explain that the director is responsible for coordinating the entire production. He or she reviews scripts, checks to see that graphics are made, schedules taping sessions, and notifies the crew. Have the students elect a director for the month's project. Ask for volunteers for the other tasks. Explain that there will be a variety of activities taped and that they will need four people for each of the remaining tasks.

Conduct a brainstorming session with the entire group to gather ideas about activities to videotape for the monthly school news program. Have the director make notes of the suggestions. Planning should include the entire crew to give the students serving as technicians input as well as a sense of purpose and direction. This also encourages students to exchange roles, sometimes operating cameras, other times making graphics or interviewing.

Ask the director to read the list of suggested topics and to have the group choose four to videotape. Have the students choose the one they would like to work on for the next session.

Session III—Duplicate script planning sheets as shown here:

Audio	Video

Have the director read the four activities that will be featured on the monthly news program. Have the students volunteer for production tasks for each segment. Five students will be on each crew, plus the director coordinating the entire program.

Have the crews meet separately to plan the videotaping of their particular activity. Direct the students to determine an overall purpose for the segment to give them a sense of direction. Explain that the camera person and the audio person need to understand the purpose of the tape as well as the talent or reporter. Better videotapes result when the talent and the technicians plan ahead what the segment will look like when completed.

Explain that some scripting is necessary, but loose scripting seems to be most useful. Explain that scripts contain audio and video directions. Distribute the script sheets to each group. In an interview, questions should be formulated and video directions established, but it is important for the reporter to listen and react to the replies to questions. Avoid reading from the script. Try to maintain a quality of spontaneity, which gives a freshness and lifelike quality to the piece.

Provide time for students to plan videotaping segments. Planning should include any graphics, such as titles, charts, or still illustrations, that will be needed. Graphics should be prepared by the following session.

Session IV—Provide an opportunity for each crew to go over their script with the entire group, describing both audio and video directions and showing graphics to be used. Have the students make comments and give suggestions on each segment.

Discuss instructions for videotaping. Explain that editing is a time-consuming, tedious process that often results in a disappointing finished product. Tell the students that one of their goals when videotaping is to have very little editing work to be done. Caution students to make a test run before taping to be certain all equipment is working properly. While taping, remind them not to move the camera too much. Zooming is fun but it makes viewers dizzy. Be sure lighting is adequate. Whenever possible, retape if a significant error is made.

Ask the crews to videotape their segments under the supervision of the director, who will schedule and be present at all taping sessions. All videotaping should be completed by the next session.

Have the students gather in groups of five to read and to interpret their bibliographies.

Follow-up: Direct the students to make final copies of their bibliographies to be submitted with their reports.

This activity should be planned for all students the first time a bibliography is required at this level. Encourage students to request further assistance in compiling bibliographies whenever needed. Instruct students who have not mastered the skill individually or in small groups.

SAMPLE BIBLIOGRAPHY ON PHOTOGRAPHY

(Book, one author)
> Siegel, Beatrice. *An Eye on the World: Margaret Bourke-White, Photographer*. New York: Frederick Warne, 1980.

(Book, two authors)
> Lathrop, Irvin T. and Marshall LaCour. *Basic Book of Photography*. Chicago: American Technical Society, 1979.

(Book, more than two authors)
> Graves, Ken, et al. *American Snapshots*. San Francisco, California: Scrimshaw Press, 1977.

(Book, editor)
> Lahue, Kalton, ed. *Petersen's Big Book of Photography*. New York: Petersen Publishing Co., 1977.

(Encyclopedia, general unsigned)
> "Photography," *The World Book Encyclopedia*. Chicago: World Book-Childcraft International, Inc., 1981.

(Encyclopedia, general signed)
> Morgan, Willard D. and John S. Carroll. "Photography," *Colliers Encyclopedia*. New York: Macmillan Educational Corporation, 1981, v. 18.

(Encyclopedia, subject unsigned)
> "Color Film Processing," *Encyclopedia of Practical Photography*. Garden City, New York: American Photographic Book Publishing Company, 1978, v. 3.

(Encyclopedia, subject signed)
> Klick, Clifford and James H. Schulman. "Photography," *McGraw-Hill Encyclopedia of Science and Technology*, 1978, v. 10.

(Magazine, unsigned)
> "Make Winter Photography a Snap," *Seventeen*. December 1980.

(Magazine, signed)
> Hurter, William. "Zeroing in on Color Balance," *Petersen's Photographic*. May 1980.

(Newspaper, unsigned)
> "Ansel Adams is named honorary member of Moscow's commission on graphic artists," *The New York Times*. February 22, 1978.

(Newspaper, signed)
> Perry, Robin, "Creative Use of Wide Angle and Telephoto Lenses," *The New York Times*. May 10, 1981.

(Pamphlet)
> *Photographic Equipment Techniques*. Moravia, New York: Chronicle Guidance Publications, 1980.

(Audiovisual Materials)
> *Photography-The Creative Eye: Effective Darkroom Techniques*.
> (Sound slide/cassette) White Plains, New York: The Center for Humanities, Inc., 1979.

(Television Program)
> *Ansel Adams: Photographer*. Filmamerica, Inc., 1981. Aired on PBS, May 13, 1981.

(Microform)
> "Pulitzer Prize to Joe Rosenthal," *The New York Times School Microfilm Collection*. May 8, 1945, reel 133.

TV MATERIALS

This activity provides opportunities to interpret what is seen and heard. It encourages students to recall, summarize, paraphrase, and extend what is listened to and viewed.

Time: 40 minutes

Materials: Materials from the library media center collection that relate to recent television programs

Preparation: Prepare a display of library media center materials that relate to recent television programs. Include items from the fiction and non-fiction collections, as well as magazines, newspapers, and a list of pertinent audiovisual materials. Also include a television program schedule with recommended programs circled in red pencil.

Activity Directions:

Give a book talk surveying the displayed materials that relate to recent television programs. Briefly describe the materials, highlighting the way each extends the content of the corresponding television program.

Discuss the difference between reading and viewing. Develop the concept that viewing provides a visual image that often increases understanding. Viewing often provides an introduction to a new topic or idea. Reading provides more in-depth coverage, which may be paced at the rate of the reader's thought. Point out the necessity for both kinds of media.

Ask the students to consider the difference between viewing fiction television and nonfiction television. Develop the concept that when viewing fiction television the experience and feelings at the time that the program is seen are the main emphasis. In nonfiction television, the information that is given by the program or remembered after the viewing is most significant. Point out that the viewer must pay different types of attention in each case.

Have the students describe how they could use the library media center materials to follow up fiction and nonfiction television programs. Develop an understanding that after a fiction program they might want to read a book on which the program was based, or a book in a similar genre, or something about a problem or idea presented. In nonfiction television, they might want to extend their understanding and knowledge of a topic, idea, event, or person introduced. Explain that library media center materials can provide background and in-depth information to give them a more complete understanding of the information presented in a television program.

Encourage the students to read the materials on display and to discuss both the television programs and the reading.

Follow-up: Change the display monthly with materials that relate to current television programs. You might want to have a group of students be responsible for the display.

Variations: Provide an opportunity for groups of students to meet to discuss television programs that they view and their related readings.